Building
Strong
People

Books by Bobbie Reed

Pleasing You Is Destroying Me
Prescription for a Broken Heart
Creative Bible Learning—Adult (with M. Marlowe)
Making the Most of Single Life
Too Close, Too Soon (with Jim Talley)
Dear Lord, I Can't Do It All!
Merging Families
The Single Adult Journey
The Single Parent Journey
Life after Divorce
Longing for a Child
How to Have a Healthy Family Even in Stressful Times
Surviving Your Child's Dating Years
Ministry with Single Adults Today
Listen to the Heart

Books by John Westfall

Coloring outside the Lines
Enough Is Enough

Building Strong People

How to Lead Effectively

Bobbie Reed
and
John Westfall

Foreword by
John C. Maxwell

 Baker Books

A Division of Baker Book House Co
Grand Rapids, Michigan 49516

©1997 by Network of Single Adult Leaders

Published by Baker Books
a division of Baker Book House Company
P.O. Box 6287, Grand Rapids, MI 49516-6287

Printed in the United States of America

For information about academic books, resources for Christian leaders, and all new releases available from Baker Book House, visit our web page at http://www.bakerbooks.com/

Library of Congress Cataloging-in-Publication Data
Reed, Bobbie.
    Building strong people : how to lead effectively / Bobbie Reed and John Westfall.
        p. cm.
    ISBN 0-8010-9028-8 (paper)
    1. Christian leadership. 2. Church management. I. Westfall, John. II. Title.
BV652.1.R44 1997
253—dc21
                               96-52301

Unless otherwise indicated, Scripture quotations are taken from the HOLY BIBLE, NEW INTERNATIONAL VERSION®. NIV®. Copyright ©1973, 1978, 1984 by International Bible Society. Used by permission of Zondervan Publishing House. All rights reserved.

Scripture quotations marked NASB are taken from the New American Standard Bible, © the Lockman Foundation 1960, 1962, 1963, 1968, 1971, 1972, 1973, 1975, 1977, 1995.

Scripture quotations marked TLB are taken from *The Living Bible,* copyright © 1971 by Tyndale House Publishers, Wheaton, Illinois. Used by permission.

Scripture quotation marked KJV is taken from the King James Version.

To the single adults in my life who taught me to let go.

John

To Doug Arnold, a leader who inspired each of us to stretch beyond our comfort zones to become more than we dreamed.

Bobbie

Contents

Foreword

No leader can work alone. By definition a *leader* is someone who leads others. A leader, therefore, has followers. But in ministry today, the goal of a leader goes beyond having followers; the goal is to develop strong followers into effective leaders and team members.

The first responsibility of a leader is to recognize potential leadership ability in others. Too often we see people as they are and not as they could be. Yet when people sense that someone believes in them, they instinctively respond and strive to fulfill that person's trust in them. People grow toward the expectations of the one who believes in them. Strong leaders have learned to expect great things from others, to clearly communicate those expectations, and to affirm potential leaders as they work toward those expectations. People need recognition not only of their successes but also of their willingness to take the risks involved in practicing new and unfamiliar skills. Good leaders have learned the value of praise, affirmation, and sharing the credit for a job well done.

The second responsibility of a leader is to create an atmosphere that attracts potential leaders and that allows them to develop their leadership abilities. Creating such a climate in which leaders can develop is a win-win situation. The primary leader benefits because the burden of the job is shared. The potential leader benefits by being allowed to grow and develop in a safe environment. The organization benefits because the work is being done on a timely basis by a team. When there is a leadership team, team members look out for, care for, assist, and provide honest feedback to one another.

Basically, potential leaders need to be exposed to successful leaders, provided a secure environment for risk taking, mentored by an experienced leader, given needed tools and resources, and trained in appropriate skills. However, to help individual leaders grow and develop, the climate must be altered to meet the needs of the individual leaders being developed. Some will need emotional support, others skills training. Most will need financial resources, equipment, and support personnel.

The third responsibility of a leader is to have a vision and to encourage others to develop a sense of vision. True leaders are never satisfied with things as they are. Like John F. Kennedy, they do not just see things as they are but they see things as they could be and ask, "Why not?" They are constantly breaking new ground, conquering new worlds, and moving away from what is and what has always been. Great leaders are always looking for ways to increase performance and to encourage others to stretch their comfort zones and to become more than they are. Leaders share their dreams and encourage potential leaders to share, and then to strive toward, their own dreams.

The fourth responsibility of a leader is to know when it is time to let go and delegate to the potential leaders. A leader who has not learned this lesson is restricted by the constraints of time, energy, ability, and vision to what he or she can do alone, as one person. A leader who has learned to let go finds that the boundaries of ministry are removed, and the achievement potential seems unlimited as more and more people are allowed to dream and to participate in making the dreams come true.

This book helps leaders with these four responsibilities and shows how to be leaders of leaders, dream releasers, and kingdom builders.

Dr. John C. Maxwell
Founder of INJOY, Inc.
Author of *Developing the Leaders around You* and
Developing the Leader within You

Introduction

There is a great deal of confusion among church leaders about their roles. There is often a belief that they are expected to be managers, to be efficient, effective, and resourceful in managing God's resources as administered by the local church. Certainly there is need for management some of the time but all too often we step in and try to help God "do it better," never realizing or knowing the damage we can cause in the lives of others. We have taken care of people and "done it for them" so long that we have created congregations of people who are passive, dependent, uninspired, inhibited, and uncreative.

There is a need to rediscover an enabling style of leadership as an approach to ministry so that people can be released to minister in the power of the Holy Spirit.

The key concept of this book is the answer to the question, Is it my job to build a strong ministry or is it to build strong people who minister? We believe that if we build strong people who minister, then our ministries will be strong. But if we strive to build strong ministries, we may end up not building strong people.

There is a leadership assessment at the end of this introduction that will assist you in determining your preferred style and in determining which phase of your ministry (philosophy, planning, organizing, implementing, or evaluating) needs changes.

If you are willing to build leaders by responding to their needs, drawing out their dreams, and equipping and empowering them, you will become a true leader yourself. Sometimes that means letting go and staying out of the way so that God can work in a fresh way to further his ministry.

Self-Assessment Tool

What's Your Leadership Quotient?

Read each of the situations given in this assessment and rate all of the possible responses using the following ratings:

10 = The one response completely characteristic of you

7 = The one response somewhat characteristic of you

4 = The one response somewhat uncharacteristic of you

1 = The one response completely uncharacteristic of you

This is a forced choice assessment. You can use the above responses only once in each situation, which means that you will score one of the four responses as a 10, one as a 7, one as a 4, and one as a 1. Sometimes the choice will be difficult as perhaps none of the responses are completely characteristic (or uncharacteristic) of you, but choose the ones that come closest.

I. Philosophy of Ministry

Your philosophy of ministry will determine the way you carry out programs, recruit and train staff, and spend your time.

A. What do you view as your primary role as a leader?

_____1. I think my job is to build a strong ministry that helps heal hurting people.

_____2. I think my job is to build up and equip people so they can minister to one another.

_____3. I think my job is to do whatever is necessary (whatever isn't getting done) to ensure that the ministry is successful.

_____4. I think my job is to try and keep the senior pastor/staff/congregation/board pleased with the programs we provide.

B. What is the goal of your ministry?

_____1. To not upset the congregation.

_____2. To provide a full range of successful and effective programs.

_____3. To provide a place of ministry.

_____4. To develop people into ministers.

C. What place does creativity have in your ministry?

_____1. I sometimes think people try to be too creative and are easily bored.

_____2. I spend a lot of time thinking up creative ideas for our ministry.

_____3. I give my leaders the freedom to explore and implement their own creative ideas.

_____4. I listen to creative ideas, evaluate them, ensure that they are compatible with our programs, and give my approval when appropriate.

II. Planning

Once the mission or overall goal of the ministry has been agreed on, the programs and activities that fulfill that goal must be planned.

A. How do you plan the monthly calendar?

___1. I carefully plan it so it is balanced for everyone's needs. I make copies and ensure that everyone gets a copy so they will know what is happening.

___2. Our calendar is basically the same each month. Why change what is working well?

___3. I meet with the various leaders each month and together we develop the monthly calendar as a team.

___4. I have a set criteria for the monthly calendar (a balanced percentage of socials, Bible study, and ministry projects), which the various leaders follow. They submit a draft calendar to me each month, which I then review and either approve or modify as needed.

B. How do you train your staff?

___1. I assess the individual training needs of each leader and provide opportunities for growth and learning (e.g., on-the-job training, classes, reading, and trying new skills).

___2. I send leaders to training conferences and workshops when possible and sometimes I even teach the classes myself.

___3. I work individually with the various leaders and have them observe me while I show them how to do a task/activity they want to learn how to do.

___4. If someone asks me how to do something, I am happy to tell them.

C. How do you solve problems?
___1. My people bring me a problem and a recommended solution, which I evaluate and either accept or reject. If I reject it, I have them make another recommendation.
___2. I meet with people and we discuss the problem, explore alternatives, and work together until we develop a successful solution.
___3. I've found that when problems are big enough usually my senior pastor/staff/congregation/board come and tell me what to do about them. Basically I can ignore the minor problems because they'll resolve themselves.
___4. I analyze the problem, determine the cause, develop the best alternative, and inform the group how I'm going to solve the problem.

III. Organizing

Each ministry needs some degree of organization to facilitate its operation.
A. How are staff duties defined in your ministry?
___1. When a new leader is recruited, I spend some time with him/her and we discuss the role and how it fits into the overall program. Together we agree on what roles and responsibilities he/she will be accountable for.
___2. Most people have their own ideas about how they want to do a job, and I let them do it their way unless they ask for help.
___3. I do most of the important tasks in the ministry so I can be sure everything is handled appropriately and done successfully. Sometimes I let one of the leaders assist me.
___4. I have a complete set of organization charts and prepared duty statements for each position in

the ministry. When a new leader is recruited, I give him/her a copy to sign and return to me and one to keep so he/she knows what's expected of him/her.

B. How rigid are your operational procedures?

____1. I do all of the paperwork (transportation requests, purchase requisitions, attendance reports, etc.) to ensure that we comply with our operational procedures.

____2. I've developed several logs and forms to simplify obtaining approvals and tracking projects. I make sure everyone is aware of and follows the appropriate procedures.

____3. We have written operational procedures, but they are changed whenever we discover a better and easier way to do a task/activity and still maintain the necessary degree of accountability.

____4. We don't have many written procedures. We just "play it by ear." We deal with problems as they arise.

C. Describe the chain of command in your ministry and how it works.

____1. We don't have a set chain of command, actually. Anyone can confer with anyone else and make the necessary decisions.

____2. I have several subordinate leaders I am developing. They are responsible for developing other leaders. However, for basic communication, my door is open to anyone.

____3. We have a fully developed organization chart (pyramid style) and the span of control is carefully planned. I have only two to four people who report to and deal directly with me. I insist people work through the chain of command for decisions and communication.

_____4. Basically everyone reports to me, and I try to make time to meet with and make decisions for every subordinate leader.

IV. Implementation

Making a plan become a reality requires a lot of effort and activity.

A. How do you recruit leaders for your programs?

_____1. People volunteer themselves.

_____2. I actively recruit by contacting people individually and selling them on the job.

_____3. I evaluate candidates against the leadership qualification requirements we have set.

_____4. I pray that God will send me people to do the tasks and commit myself to assist in their development into strong leaders. (I also pray that God will give me the vision to see in them what he sees in them, for sometimes this is hard to do!)

B. How do you communicate with the singles and singles leaders?

_____1. Mostly in writing (memos, policies, procedures, bulletins).

_____2. I answer any questions I'm asked.

_____3. Mostly in meetings (regular planning; weekly sessions; ad hoc groups; impromptu, as-needed gatherings).

_____4. At regular sessions, I go around and talk to people one-to-one and be sure that everyone gets the necessary information.

C. How do you coordinate a new program?

___1. I have leaders carefully outline the new program and give me a written plan with time frames and deadlines, which I then monitor to ensure success.

___2. I provide encouragement, affirmation, feedback, support, and assistance to the new leader.

___3. I take charge for the first two to four weeks of any new program to be sure our plans are good and there won't be major problems.

___4. I let the leaders follow their own ideas/plans unless a major problem arises.

V. Evaluation

There comes a time to evaluate how the ministry is doing.

A. How do you evaluate your ministry?

___1. The first step in our regular planning session is to discuss the previous period's (month, quarter) activities and evaluate how effectively we've met our goals.

___2. I observe the ministry programs and the leaders while they are ministering and in our staff meetings.

___3. We know we're not successful if there is a lack of participation or if the senior pastor/staff/congregation/board wants something changed.

___4. I have leaders submit quarterly reports of various elements (attendance, results, meetings held, feedback from participants) and meet with each one to discuss his/her success.

B. When do you evaluate?

___1. On a set periodic schedule (quarterly, semiannually, etc.) and after each new event.

   2. When a leader has tried a new skill, task, or responsibility, to provide feedback to him/her on his/her development.

   3. Continually, every day, at every event I attend. I am always making notes.

   4. Whenever I need to submit a report to the senior pastor/staff/congregation/board or to justify a purchase or budget increase.

C. How do you evaluate your leaders?

   1. I write lengthy performance evaluations and outline each area that needs attention; then I meet individually with each one and discuss the evaluation.

   2. I evaluate them against their written goals and give written feedback on a set periodic schedule.

   3. I evaluate the degree to which, in my opinion, each leader has grown spiritually and developed new skills. I ask the person to share how he/she thinks he/she has grown and I give my observations. Together we either reconfirm the set objective for personal growth or set a new one.

   4. If people ask me how they are doing, I give them my opinion.

Scoring Form

Step 1

In the spaces below, write the rating numbers that correspond to your responses on the assessment. For example, for I-A, first fill in the rating you gave yourself for question 2, then for question 1, and so forth. It may look like this:

I-A   2. <u>10</u> 1. <u>7</u> 3. <u>4</u> 4. <u>1</u>

Please note that the responses are not in numerical order. After you have entered all of the ratings, subtotal and total the ratings where indicated.

	Leader	Manager	Worker	Reactor
Philosophy				
I-A	2. ____	1. ____	3. ____	4. ____
I-B	4. ____	2. ____	3. ____	1. ____
I-C	3. ____	4. ____	2. ____	1. ____
Subtotal	____	____	____	____
Planning				
II-A	3. ____	4. ____	1. ____	2. ____
II-B	1. ____	2. ____	3. ____	4. ____
II-C	2. ____	1. ____	4. ____	3. ____
Subtotal	____	____	____	____
Organizing				
III-A	1. ____	4. ____	3. ____	2. ____
III-B	3. ____	2. ____	1. ____	4. ____
III-C	2. ____	3. ____	4. ____	1. ____
Subtotal	____	____	____	____
Implementing				
IV-A	4. ____	3. ____	2. ____	1. ____
IV-B	3. ____	1. ____	4. ____	2. ____
IV-C	2. ____	1. ____	3. ____	4. ____
Subtotal	____	____	____	____
Evaluating				
V-A	1. ____	4. ____	2. ____	3. ____
V-B	2. ____	1. ____	4. ____	3. ____
V-C	3. ____	2. ____	1. ____	4. ____
Subtotal	____	____	____	____
Grand Totals	____	____	____	____

Step 2

Chart your scores on the graphs provided on page 23 by finding the number corresponding to your score for leader (L) on the vertical axis and then making a dot at that point on the L line. After you have plotted each component, connect the dots and compare the result with the "ideal" graph line. The significance of the results will be discussed later in the book.

Graphs of component scores showing distribution of scores

I. Philosophy

II. Planning

III. Organizing

IV. Implementing

V. Evaluating

Grand Total

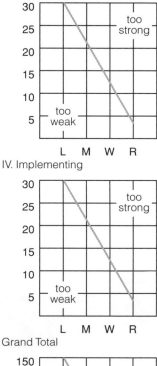

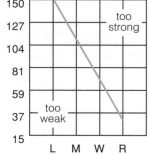

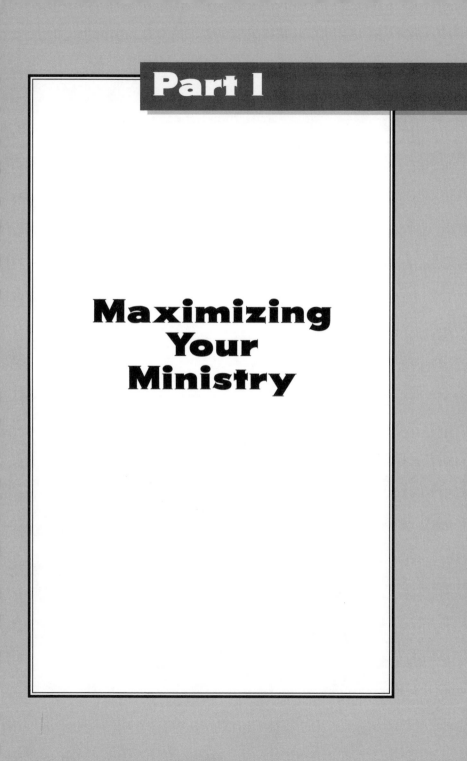

Part I

Maximizing Your Ministry

Purpose

What Am I Doing Here?

ill was sick. It was late Saturday night and he had the flu and was tired but valiantly he kept trying to focus his attention on preparation for the class he was to teach in the morning. Suddenly the phone rang. It was Paul Wilson (senior pastor at the church where Bill served as associate pastor). "I heard that you're sick. Do yourself a favor and don't come to church tomorrow," he said. Bill was touched by the pastor's concern but knew that he had to be there for he was teaching an adult education class that had more than three hundred members. It was crucial that he be there; they needed him, and no one else could possibly teach that class on such short notice. After all, it was Saturday night.

Despite Bill's protests, the pastor insisted that Bill call a few class members and turn over the responsibility of teaching to them. "Who knows," he chuckled, "it might just be the best class they've ever had."

Reluctantly Bill called the first leader who came to mind. Karen said not to worry, she would call a few others and together they would put together something to salvage the class. A group of leaders gathered, planned a small group discussion and Bible study, developed a teaching strategy, and led the class . . . without Bill. Sunday afternoon Bill got the report, "It was the best class we've ever had!"

He was glad that everything worked out so well but inside he had a nagging sense of fear and doubt. What if they don't need me? What am I doing here?

What's the Goal?

After feeling sorry for himself for a suitable length of time, Bill began to realize that the people did need him. They needed him to do exactly what he had done in getting out of the way and giving them an opportunity to stretch and grow and minister to each other. We also may need to rethink our goals for ministry.

Key Questions:
Is it our goal to build strong ministries?
Or, is it our goal to build strong people who minister?

Depending on which of these goals we are committed to, we will automatically allocate our time, energies, and activities in one of two directions: toward completing the task or toward developing people.

If we are focused on completing the task, some people will probably develop new skills in the process, but those skills will be at a minimal level. If we focus on developing people, the task will probably get done but not necessarily the way we may have had in mind. We get to choose which outcome is more important to us.

Building a Strong Ministry

Choosing isn't all that easy. Leaders who value task completion have the satisfaction of developing and running well-planned programs. The results are clearly and immediately measurable in terms of numbers of meetings, classes or services held, attendance figures, and compliments received. "You did well," people will say at the end of the event.

On the other hand, leaders who value developing people may have to wait longer to experience satisfaction. People develop new skills slowly, as they learn and practice new skills in ministering and relating to one another. On some days you may even wonder if you are making a difference in anyone's life because progress seems so slow. But when we do note the progress and see people changing around us, it is exciting to remember that we had a part in their development. After a major breakthrough, people will say to their leader, "I never thought I could do it."

When we look at the results in people's lives, we may find it easier to choose the goal for our ministry.

An emphasis on task completion—on building strong ministries—produces followers. The people will tend to be:

- passive—waiting to be told what to believe, think, or do
- dependent—waiting for the leader to do everything
- bored—waiting for the leader to do something
- weak—waiting to be rescued
- critical—waiting to find fault and place blame

Recently a person stepped forward and was given responsibility to coordinate a citywide luncheon where a nationally known leader was going to speak on how members of the body of Christ are to relate in ministry.

Eager to do the best job possible, she spent many hours planning the menu and place settings with the caterer, decorating the meeting hall, advertising the event, and ensuring that nothing would go wrong. The deadline for reservations had been set for 9:00 on the Monday morning before the Friday meeting. She was indignant that many people had registered at the last moment and even past the deadline, but she was finally persuaded to go ahead and at least allow these less than "responsible" people to attend. However, they were not allowed to eat with those who had registered on time and they would have to sit in chairs lined up around the back of the room. She then made different-color name tags so that she could easily determine who had prepaid and who had missed the cutoff date.

The luncheon was an operational success. There was no confusion about who had or hadn't registered on time or who was eating and who was not. The food was excellent and the room looked fabulous. However, in the process of putting on a successful program, the leader forgot the effect her system would have on the people. Many of the participants who registered late felt belittled, alienated, left out, and unwelcome.

Building Strong People

An emphasis on building strong people who minister produces leaders. The people will tend to be:

- active—ready to take risks in order to grow
- independent—ready to take on the work of the ministry
- enthusiastic—ready to dream beyond the practical
- courageous—ready to reach out to others in pain

- understanding—ready to be vulnerable, accountable, aware of their own pain and that of others

Charles had just started a new young adult program in his church and things were going surprisingly well after only a few weeks. One day several members of the group came and asked if they could have a retreat. Immediately he told them all of the roadblocks that he could think of off the top of his head and eloquently (he thought) expressed the rationale for waiting several months before attempting such an industrious undertaking. They wanted to have the retreat the next month. He patiently explained how they would need more time to plan because no facility would be available on such short notice and they could never get a decent speaker in time.

None of his discouraging logic slowed them down in any way and soon they were hard at work planning their retreat. They found an available ski lodge (that was way too expensive) three hours away (much too far). One of the leaders agreed to lead the singing (but he knew only two chords on the guitar and everyone knows that Christian music requires at least three chords!). Without a special guest speaker, the group selected some of its members to teach and lead discussions and small groups, while others planned recreational and team-building activities.

Driving up the mountain to the retreat, Charles was fully prepared to offer encouragement at what he expected was going to be a total disaster but still an opportunity for his people to learn a lesson through their bitter failure. Arriving at the lodge, he was surprised to see that the building was packed and overflowing with enthusiastic young adults. For the entire three days he had a terrible migraine headache, worrying about what might go wrong, but to this day people look back and remember the event as the "best retreat we ever had." Perhaps the program wasn't the best by some standards but the participants felt included, important, involved, and cared for.

Another example is the first single adult Sunday school class at a little church in Fair Oaks, California. There were only eight members and they met in the choir dressing room. Each member was struggling with the realities of being single again, some with children. Although there was a curriculum for the class to study, there were some weeks that they never made it to the lesson. Sessions started with sharing about the week, and if a person was in a particularly difficult place right then, the class would take time to listen, encourage, pray for, and hug that person. Although some members were stronger than others, over a period of several months, each person had occasion to be ministered to by the group. Task completers might criticize such a class because they didn't stick to the prepared lesson. People developers could cheer the class leader who dared to allow ministry to take place.

The Challenge

When we decide to pursue the goal of developing people first and foremost, a series of specific choices will follow.

1. Choosing to draw people into circles. The challenge of leadership is to be willing to go where people are. The leader draws a circle of people around himself or herself before releasing them to go draw circles of people around them. This may be contrary to our natural inclinations to seek and hoard power for ourselves. Some people are like spiritual Sumo wrestlers, who beef up spiritually and expend their energies attempting to knock others out of the circle. Jesus' method was the opposite of this. He moved toward people, drawing them into his circle or drawing himself into their circle of life.

One way to draw people into relationship circles is to encourage them to join small fellowship or study groups. However, some people may resist this approach. Many people don't feel comfortable with the intimacy, vulnerability, and accountability of belonging to a small group. There are people in our lives and in our churches whose basic goal is to hide out. Our challenge is to create a safe environment for relating so people can dare to risk being vulnerable with us.

Some people come to church because they are hurting; others come to cover up their pain with a spiritual Band-Aid. Some come to get involved, others to retreat from life. Some come to give, others to receive. Whatever the initial motivation people have for coming to the church, our challenge is to be the facilitator for their development. The best way to do this is to be in relationship with them and to be open and honest about who we are. When we draw people into our circle, we begin the relationship process.

2. Choosing to grow ourselves. We must each ask the question, "What is God calling me to be?" As a member of a small group we become vulnerable and risk exposure of not only our strengths but also our flaws. We risk having to face the need and the decision to change. In the process of releasing others to minister, we often give up the spotlight, the recognition, the immediate satisfaction of being the one who got it done. Our challenge is to become aware of our own needs for development and in the process of helping others grow, find ourselves growing.

3. Choosing to trust God. When we think of beginning a new program, we usually start looking for the "right" person to be responsible for the program. By the right person, we usually mean someone who is skilled enough to make the program successful according to our standards and agendas. We select the good speaker to teach, the gifted musician to lead singing, the accountant to handle the finances, and the grandmother to provide child care. We end up with a successful program—and with people neatly pigeonholed so they cannot grow or function outside of their comfort zone. While it is appropriate for people to use their gifts in ministry, it is also important to involve people whose gifts have not yet been fully developed.

Perhaps a little "fruitbasket upset" (remember the youth group game) with people would allow us to move beyond our predictable, controlled ways. Perhaps the grandmother has wisdom to share, even if she can't speak comfortably in front of three or four hundred people. Perhaps the musician would like to help in ways unrelated to music. Perhaps God has brought to your church someone he'd like you to develop for ministry. By looking for only those who fit our images of the "right" people, we may not see God's choice for the position. We have to be willing to take people as they are with their own unique dreams, styles, idiosyncrasies, sins, fatal flaws, gifts, and talents and encourage them to stretch in new areas and explore opportunities to minister.

Bob was a seminar leader who met a woman who had been through an overwhelming number of life shocks and was nearly devastated and immobilized. The woman shared that she had a dream that God would allow her to use what she had learned through her pain to lead seminars someday. She had been a women's Bible study leader for several years and indicated that she loved teaching and speaking.

After hearing her story Bob invited her to come with him to assist in leading his next seminar, which was to be at a very large and prominent church. The woman was ecstatic and spent two weeks preparing for her part of the seminar. Everything went wrong. She showed up dressed embarrassingly inappropriately. Her thoughts were disjointed and seemingly unfocused on the topic of the seminar, and her comments were confusing. Bob was completely surprised by the inadequate presentation. He had assumed she would do a good job but realized, too late, that he should have assisted her in her preparation. Following the sessions, the pastor approached Bob privately and asked why in the world he had associated himself with such a person and risked his own reputation as a seminar leader.

Although Bob was never asked to return to that church (where he had done annual seminars for the previous five years), he continued to let the woman participate in his seminars. With practice she became skilled in focusing her thoughts and sharing what God had done in her life. Her story became effective because Bob was willing to risk himself, to let go of the task-completion attitude, and to facilitate another person's growth. Today the woman conducts very effectively her own seminars throughout the country.

The challenges are great but the rewards are greater. What are we here for? We are here to be conduits of God's love and facilitators of individual growth (our own and that of others).

Perspective

What Is My Style?

Note: If you haven't completed and scored the self-assessment tool in the introduction to discover your leadership quotient, do so now.

There are four approaches to ministry that we will be discussing in this book: *leading, managing, working,* and *reacting*. Each of us has developed a preference for one of these approaches based on our success with that style in the past. Every person will probably use each of the four approaches at different times. In this book, we will show why we believe "leading" should be the main approach to ministry.

First, let's define each approach.

Reacting

Sam Williams is a reactor. He waits until something absolutely must be done or changed before taking action. His response to suggestions to change or improve a program is usually negative. But he does respond to pressure, criticism, demands, and suggestions from people in authority and when reacting will often overcorrect the situation. Sam is basically a procrastinator, and underlying his approach may be a fear of risking or being criticized. He has few established operational procedures and a very loose system of accountability.

While each of us must be open and responsive to the input of others, we don't want to spend more than about 5 percent of our time to make more than about 5 percent of our decisions based solely on the opinions and demands of others. If we do, we are letting other people set our schedule, goals, and priorities.

The beliefs behind this approach are:

1. If it's not broken, don't fix it.
2. If something is seriously wrong, people will let me know.
3. Some problems go away if they are ignored long enough.
4. Making a mistake is almost unforgivable.
5. If it's someone else's idea, I won't be blamed if it doesn't work out.
6. Success is keeping people happy.

People usually respond to this approach by:

1. Becoming frustrated and bored.
2. Learning to complain loudly to get results.
3. Ganging up on the person in charge to force action or decisions.
4. Making changes themselves and not always telling the person in charge.
5. Considering the reactor to be weak and ineffective.
6. Not being happy.

Working

Betty Phillips is a worker. She does things all by herself. No job is too menial; if there is no one else to do something, Betty will do it, without even looking for someone to whom to delegate. At meetings she makes the coffee, brings the donuts, sets up the chairs, checks the sound system and room temperature, hands out the bulletins (which she writes, types, copies, and folds), leads the singing, and teaches the lesson. After the session she greets people, counsels when necessary, cleans up the room, and locks up when everyone else leaves. Betty is usually busy, tired, and often impatient with people who are not racing around at her same speed. She has difficulty saying no to the demands of others and can almost always fit one more thing into her schedule.

While we need to be willing to support the program by helping out wherever help is needed, we don't want to spend more than about 15 percent of our time and energies being workers. Whenever we as leaders take on a task of ministry we are actually depriving someone else of the opportunity to be involved in ministry.

The beliefs behind this approach are:

1. Everything must be done and done right.
2. I can do it better than anyone else.
3. People can't be trusted to follow through.
4. Nobody is willing to help.
5. Working is more fun than relating.
6. Success is doing a good job.

People usually respond to this approach by:

1. Letting the worker do all the work.
2. Criticizing what doesn't go well.

3. Not taking responsibility for themselves or the program.
4. Not following through on commitments.
5. Appreciating the worker.
6. Enjoying their comfort zones instead of stretching and growing.

Managing

Tyrone Jenner is a manager. He gets the job done (his way) through others. Tyrone relies on his skills in planning, organizing, directing, controlling, monitoring, and evaluating. While Tyrone seeks the input of others and has a truly participative style of management, he still retains the ultimate responsibility for making decisions. Tyrone encourages his people to be creative in recommending solutions to problems and ideas for new programs but everything must be cleared through him and have his approval before implementation.

Tyrone is somewhat of a bottleneck, although he tries hard to expedite paperwork and decisions. He tries to find just the right person with the perfect skills for a task and recruits that person to use talents and gifts doing what he or she does best. He has written many operational procedures, developed teaching tools, and designed various forms to use in his projects. Tyrone is skilled in the latest time-management techniques and lives and dies by his schedule.

While we cannot avoid managerial duties some of the time, we must recognize that if more than 40 percent of our time is spent managing, we may be putting the program ahead of people.

The beliefs behind this approach are:

1. People and programs need to be managed or controlled.
2. The more efficient you are, the better it is.
3. Measurable results are critical.
4. I must plan ways to meet everyone's needs.
5. People must not fail, so I must rescue them if failure threatens.
6. Success is having a smooth-running program.

People usually respond to this approach by:

1. Rebelling against the rigid procedures and high expectations, or
2. Meekly following the policies and procedures.
3. Putting on efficient programs.
4. Depending on the manager for direction.
5. Remaining in their comfort zones.
6. Going outside the church to meet their needs for development.

Leading

Angie St. John is a leader. Her goal is to provide a safe environment in ministry where each participant can risk being him- or herself without fear of rejection. She is an enabler, a model, a facilitator, and a guide. Although she has a lot of creative ideas, she allows others to dream and helps them move toward realizing those dreams. Angie considers the program to be temporary and always subject to change if the needs and dreams of others change. While there are some set procedures, these are few and exist primarily to assist in helping dreams be born.

Angie used to have a need to be in charge and visible in front of the group. However, in the process of becoming a leader, a developer of others, she made a conscious choice to let go of her need for control and allow others to share both the power and the limelight. She soon discovered the truth that when we allow God to work in the lives of others through us, we usually find that he has worked in our lives as well.

While we consider leading to be the preferred approach, we cannot spend 100 percent of our time developing people because the other tasks must also be done. A good figure to aim for is to spend a minimum of 40 percent of our time and energies leading and developing people.

The beliefs behind this approach are:

1. I don't have to control everything in the ministry.
2. Failure is a stepping stone to growth.
3. Dreams grow out of needs and can be realized.
4. I can't change people but the Holy Spirit can.
5. The goal in ministry is building strong people who minister.
6. Success is seeing God at work in people's lives as they stretch and grow.

People usually respond to this approach by:

1. Being surprised when you listen and encourage their dreams.
2. Exhibiting incredible creativity.
3. Taking responsibility for the ministry.
4. Trying out new skills.

5. Becoming more open, honest, and caring.
6. Choosing to make positive, lasting life changes.

The Self-Assessment Tool

By now you should have finished filling out the self-assessment in the introduction. You should also have plotted your scores on the graphs. If you have not completed this preparation, please stop your reading and do so now, as you will want to refer to these completed forms as we review the test and what we believe it will tell you about your preferred way of relating to people in your ministry.

Five Components of Scoring

The test has five components: philosophy, planning, organizing, implementing, and evaluating. It is important to delineate stages of the process because so often we say we believe one thing yet do something quite different. You may have scored high as a leader in the philosophy component but higher as a manager in the implementation section. This test will point out the areas in which your actions may be inconsistent with your stated beliefs in the area of leadership.

After plotting your component scores on the five graphs provided, you can visually compare your pattern to the standard progression. Where your score is much below the ideal line on the graph, you are probably weak in that approach. Where your score is much above the ideal line on the graph, you are probably too strong in that approach. If you want to work toward more closely approximating the ideal progression, you may want to work first on the areas where your scores differ significantly from the standard progression.

Familiar Patterns

Below are some familiar patterns where the scores plot significantly differently from the "ideal distribution" for leader, manager, worker, reactor.

Mr. Get-It-Done

This person believes so strongly that the mission is getting the job done that his predominant style is that of being a *worker*. To this person, no one else seems to have quite enough dedication to accomplish the task, so the only alternative is to do it oneself. The second choice is to get the tasks done through others. If these approaches don't work, a leadership style is chosen. This leader isn't very influenced by the opinions of others. So the style scores are too strong in *working* and *managing* and too weak in *leading*.

Ms. Manage-by-Crises

This person has a lot of plans and procedures but seems to throw out any of these if things don't go smoothly. She is often found directing people in reorganizing, rethinking, and redesigning the ministry in response to the little "fires" that are part of any job. While there are some *leading* choices made, they are few. The style scores are too strong in *managing* and *reacting* and too weak in *leading* and *working*.

Mrs. People Pleaser

A people pleaser's primary style is that of reacting to the input, criticism, direction, and opinions of others. If something is criticized, the people pleaser will immediately start to work on getting it changed. If her efforts aren't sufficient, she will try to let others accomplish the goal but will rarely become a strong *manager* and direct the work of oth-

Familiar patterns where scores differ signigicantly from the ideal distrbution

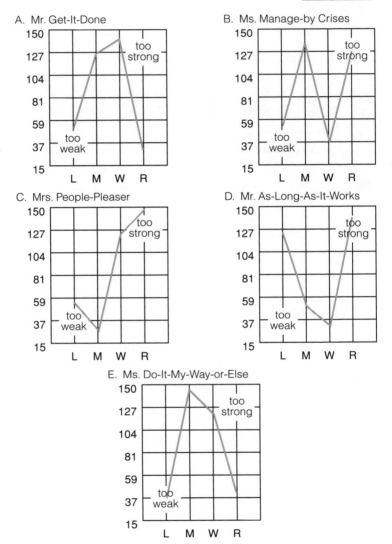

A. Mr. Get-It-Done

B. Ms. Manage-by Crises

C. Mrs. People-Pleaser

D. Mr. As-Long-As-It-Works

E. Ms. Do-It-My-Way-or-Else

ers. Her style is too strong in *reacting* and *working* and too weak in *managing* and *leading*.

Mr. As-Long-as-It-Works

This minister is primarily a *reactor* and takes the necessary action when pressured to do so by others. However, his second choice is to be a *leader*. If this doesn't work, then he will make an attempt at management and if all else fails, he will do the work. So this style is too strong in *reacting*, a little weak in *leading*, and very weak in *managing* and *working*.

Ms. Do-It-My-Way-or-Else

Her style is basically to direct the work of others and to get the job done. *Leading* and *reacting* have very little place in this style. The difference between Mr. Get-it-done and Ms. Do-it-my-way-or-else is that the first person prefers to do the work himself, while the latter will try to get the work done by others if possible.

There are many other variations of scoring patterns, but these will give you some insight into interpreting your score on the self-assessment tool. What do your scores indicate about your style? Is the pattern accurate? Will you choose to continue to follow your pattern?

Changing Approaches

In case you'd like to change or modify your approach, here are some ideas that may help.

Leader

If you are too weak

- Let other people take charge of the various ministries, retreats, meetings, etc.

- Give yourself and other people the freedom to fail.
- The next time someone brings you a problem, resist the urge to rescue him/her by solving the problem.
- The next time you are tempted to be a rescuer, don't be.
- Check your operating procedures. Are they stifling the creativity of your people? Which ones can be discarded or modified?
- Ask your leaders what their dreams are and see if you can help them realize those dreams.

Manager

If you are too weak

- Consider developing appropriate operational procedures if you don't have any.
- Find an area in which your program is failing because there is no direction. If this is a program you want to keep, temporarily take a more active role in the program development.
- If you don't have staff meetings, begin holding them.
- Take time out to meet with your leaders to evaluate your program and plan for new ministries.

Worker

If you are too weak

- Reconsider your unwillingness to do any of the actual work, then pitch in and help this week with whatever is going on.
- Take notes on how you spend your time and analyze how you can find an extra hour or two to get involved.

If you correct the areas in which you are too weak, the areas in which you are too strong will tend to self-correct. The style you use is based on a variety of factors: your skill, your history, and your success with that style. But your style can always be redecided. The choice is yours!

Process

How Am I Doing?

I just don't fit anywhere in this church," Linda explained to her pastor. "You have couples classes, a widows support group, divorce-recovery workshops, and a career singles group. My husband and I are separated and don't plan on getting divorced. I don't fit anywhere. Why aren't you meeting my needs?"

"I see what you mean," her pastor responded. "I wonder if there are any other separated people who feel the same way you do."

"Oh yes," Linda said. "I know of three others who are separated. I know they must feel as left out as I do!"

"Well, why don't you get together with them and see what you could do to meet the needs of individuals who are separated?" the pastor suggested, resisting the natural urge to immediately launch a ministry by himself—for the separated. Linda was startled at first. She had expected to share her need with the pastor and have him do something to meet it. But she was intrigued with the idea of being able to help design a new program, so she left the office determined to do it. Within a couple of weeks Linda had enlisted four other people and begun a weekly support group for the separated. From a need, a vision and a ministry were born.

Good job, pastor. You're doing just fine. You acted as a leader.

Identifying the Need

The first step in true ministry is identifying needs. We often think we know what the needs of the people are. We move from church to church duplicating programs that were a success at the last place. Sometimes they work, if the same needs exist, but sometimes they fail, because the needs are not the same. We must not presume that we automatically know the needs.

Predictable Needs

People do have similar basic needs. Sociologist Abraham Maslow grouped our primary needs into five categories: physical, security, social, self-esteem, and self-actualization. We should add a sixth category, spiritual.

Therefore, we can easily predict that the people in our congregations will have the following needs:

Needs

Physical	warmth
	comfort
	mobility
	shelter
	food
	clothing

Security	belonging to a group knowing the rules freedom from fear not having to be perfect
Social	vulnerability fellowship accountability conversation love loving others working together helping one another sharing feelings being listened to
Self-Esteem	knowing and understanding the facts receiving attention forgiveness respect courtesy acceptance praise recognition being understood ability to lead others

Self-Actualization	ability to use talents and
	   gifts
	freedom to dream and to
	   realize the dream
	daring to risk
	freedom to fail
	taking responsibility

Spiritual   knowing God
obeying God
trusting God
loving God
becoming what God
    wants you to be
sharing God with others

However, even though we can predict that people will have these needs, we don't have to rush out and start trying to fill them all at once. Most people have learned how to meet many of their own needs. Most have jobs, food, shelter, and clothing. Many do not have unreasonable fears and most have at least a few friends. So what do leaders do with the knowledge of predictable needs? They are to be aware that these needs exist and are normal. They are not surprised when occasionally one of these areas of need becomes critical in someone's life.

However, we do not need to feel pressured to develop programs to meet all of these needs because the church is not to relieve people of the responsibility for meeting their own needs. We are there to help when there is a *felt* need. We are not to follow the example of the advertising industry, which creates a need or an awareness of that need, then tries to sell us something to meet that need! Remember deodorant foot powder? Before Madison Avenue took on the challenge of marketing it, no one knew we "needed" foot powder. If our feet smelled, we washed them. However, it wasn't long before every well-appointed bathroom had a can of foot powder as a standard item!

Perceived Needs

We do encounter people who are unemployed, who have no home, and who haven't eaten in a couple of days.

There will be people who come to our churches who have no friends and who are deeply frightened by life. Often people experience a serious loss of self-esteem when they go through a rejection experience (breakup of a relationship, divorce, or separation) or lose a close friend or family member to death. Others have developed no outlet for using their natural talents and spiritual gifts. Some are starving spiritually or are spiritual babies. These people present us with opportunities for ministry. When people come to us with a complaint, our job is to help them clarify their perceived need. Sometimes people haven't taken the time to do so or they are not aware of what their real needs are. Instead they come to us angry, disappointed, hurt, or discouraged and initially all they want is to vent or complain.

Sometimes we fail by erroneously acknowledging and taking ownership of what we perceive to be felt needs. One church tried to provide a single-parent program modeled after their successful divorce-recovery program. Aware that there were twenty-five to forty single parents in the church, the associate pastor launched a "perfect" program, which balanced instruction, small group interaction, child care, and family socials. Lack of interest and poor attendance killed the program. He was puzzled. The need was there, so why didn't people respond to the program? He didn't realize that the single parents didn't feel the need that he had perceived.

In the next few months whenever single parents called in with unique needs, the pastor would give them the name and telephone number of someone who could help them. Church members who were dentists, doctors, plumbers, auto mechanics, seamstresses, and babysitters agreed to provide free checkups, alterations, tune-ups, repairs, and child care for single parents (on the basis of individual needs). People's needs were being met.

After almost a year several single parents came to the associate pastor and asked if they could start a support group and maybe have some seminars or workshops on parenting skills. This time the program succeeded because it grew out of a felt need.

Getting People to Clarify Their Needs

What are the steps in helping people to identify and clarify their needs? First, ask questions.

A good leader learns to ask a lot of questions and listens well to not only what is being said but what isn't being verbalized. When a person says, "We ought to do something to help the street people," don't just nod your head and agree. Instead, ask "How could we do that?" or "What kind of help do you think we could give?" Keep asking questions as if you were an investigative reporter. You might ask the following:

"Why do you think we should do this?" As people answer the *why* question, they may begin to reveal their own needs, hurts, disappointments, and frustrations. Discussing why we need a particular ministry may help people come to a greater understanding of themselves. It will also help you understand what is driving the complaint or request for a new ministry.

"What exactly is the need?" You will want to assist people in identifying the specific needs. "We should help the street people," might turn out to be, "It's going to drop to 20° tonight, we need to open the church for people who have no shelter." Or it might be "I met a guy outside who has no place to sleep. Can we provide three nights' lodging?"

Sometimes the expressed need isn't the true need. "We need more socials" might really be "I don't know how to make friends on a one-to-one basis, so I'm lonely."

A skilled leader learns to keep asking *what* until the real need has been defined.

"When do you experience this need?" Jenny shares, "We need a seminar on parenting skills."

Pastor asks, "When do you feel this need the most?"

"Like now," Jenny explains, "my son got into trouble yesterday in school and my daughter won't clean up her room. I just don't know what to do. I feel like such a failure!"

Jenny may need a class on parenting; however, what she probably needs more is to be in a small group where she can be affirmed, encouraged, prayed for, and nurtured. In a small group of other parents she will learn that she isn't the only parent who feels frustrated when her children don't behave the way she wants them to.

"Who is experiencing this need?" This question pinpoints the area of ministry to an individual, a family, the congregation, a portion of the congregation, or the community.

"Where do you want the need to be met?" The pastor or leader may envision the need being met at the church campus, when the person identifying the need is thinking in terms of in a home or in the community. Discussing these possibilities helps further clarify the need.

Don't Rescue People

"When someone comes into my office with a problem or a serious hurt, I've always found it is best to allow them to fully experience the pain," one pastor shares. "I provide tissues for tears but don't try to stop them."

Wise choice. Psychologists tell us that people won't change until the pain of the present situation exceeds the anticipated pain of the change process. If we step in and try to rescue people from their pain too quickly, we rob them of the greatest incentive they have to change. If someone has a need and we quickly fill it, we keep that person from the opportunity to fill that need on his or her own. Because we hate and fear pain so much, we do everything we can to avoid it or to anesthetize it. Keith Miller once wisely said that without pain, there is no wisdom. Let people experience their pain. Hurt with them. Cry with them. Don't be too quick to resolve their problems.

When we rescue people we are saying by our actions that they are dependent on us and cannot help themselves. We are sometimes stepping in and playing God, assuming that we know what is best for that person. We may enjoy the sense of being needed that comes when people are dependent on us but that isn't the basis for a healthy relationship.

Envisioning the Dream

The second step in ministry is helping people to envision their dreams. Not our dreams, their dreams! Again, just as people may not have clearly identified their needs, they also may not truly have outlined their dreams. Here are some questions to ask.

"If you feel this need, who else might also experience it?" This question broadens the dream from meeting the needs of one person to several. When the fourth person comes into your office with the same need, it may be time to get all four of them together. Perhaps a leader might tell the first person to come to him or her with a specific need to check around and to come back when three or four additional people are found who share the need and the dream.

"Where else in the world does this need exist?" This raises the need to a higher level and allows the dream to be more grandiose. A dream to meet my own needs would probably be a small dream. A dream to meet the needs of four or five would be larger, and a dream to make a difference

in my world—that's an even bigger dream. We are familiar with great leaders of the world who because they experienced deep personal needs saw a vision of a different world where those needs would be resolved for everyone. Examples include Martin Luther, Mahatma Gandhi, and Martin Luther King Jr.

One day a leader went to meet a friend for lunch. The friend worked in a high-rise in the center of town. At exactly twelve noon the elevators filled with people rushing out to find a place to eat. All over town the scene was the same. Hundreds of people rushing and never really making contact with one another. The leader was struck by how impersonal and lonely the scene was. He commented on his experience the next week in the small group that met at his house. Several people shared that they worked downtown and agreed with his assessment. Three of the people discovered that they worked in the same building in different offices and had never known it. That night a dream was born to arrange a monthly lunch for Christians who worked within a radius of a few blocks of each other. Soon there were twelve lunch clubs that were meeting regularly for fellowship and Bible study.

"If money were no object, what would your dream be?" Bobbie had sat at Bruce Larson's table for the conference luncheon. Bruce turned to her and invited her to share her dream for ministry. She did, ending with, "but that would cost a lot of money, so I don't know if I'll ever actually do it."

"Could you do it without money?" he asked gently.

Bobbie thought for a minute and realized that on a smaller scale, it could be done. "Yes," she said slowly, thoughtfully, suddenly seeing the possibilities.

"Then never let money stand in the way of your dreams," Bruce admonished.

Get people to dream the big dream as if money were no object. Then help them either find the money or scale down the dream until it is achievable. Almost every dream is possible when we approach it this way. Even expensive ones.

Actually, there is plenty of money in the world. There is sufficient money for almost all of our dreams, so the problem really isn't money. The challenge is in finding ways to access available money to fund our dreams.

"If you were an expert, what would you do?" Some people limit their ministries by thinking that they have to be experts in order to meet needs. But God uses us even when we aren't experts. We tend to want him to use us by sharing our victories, when instead he often uses our struggles.

Camilla was a seminar speaker who lectured on a variety of topics related to successful living. She was also a single parent. Churches kept asking her to speak on single parenting but she refused because she didn't feel she was totally successful in that role in spite of her best efforts. The requests persisted. Finally she agreed. At the first seminar, she was open about her own struggles, fears, insecurities, and frustrations. She also shared helpful hints about reducing sibling conflicts, finding enough time for tasks, and dealing with legal leftovers from a divorce. But it was her struggles people responded to most.

"I came to find out what I was doing wrong," one participant said, smiling through tears, "I found out I'm alright! If the 'expert' leader is struggling, then it's okay if I struggle as well!"

When people identify with us as fellow travelers, we do not have to be experts.

"What have you done before like this?" Often our dreams spring from positive similar experiences we've had. It's good to identify those and to build dreams on past successes. Often the process of implementing a dream is similar regardless of what the dream may be. You:

assess the need

get people together who share the need

brainstorm possible ways to meet the need

outline the alternatives

choose the best one

gather resources

implement the dream

evaluate the success

adjust the strategy as appropriate

Helping people see that they have used such a process successfully in the past will encourage them to believe in their abilities to make this dream work.

"What do you expect the results of this dream will be?" The time to explore expectations is before the dream is implemented. Unrealistic expectations can kill a dream before it is fully implemented. We can dream big but our expectations need to be reality based.

"What are the consequences of doing the dream as compared to not doing the dream?" Consuela had a dream. She called it "Jesus, California Style." It was a huge Christian fair. She rented the state fairgrounds, brought in singers, speakers, and exhibitors. It was the largest Christian gathering in the city that year and many found Christ during the three-day event. Everyone considered it a tremendous success. Few knew that Consuela had mortgaged her own home in order to have start-up money for her dream. Few knew the faith it took but Consuela had counted the cost and was willing to risk everything. For her the dream was worth whatever it cost.

People often need coaching in counting the cost in time, energy, money, and commitment. Sometimes people need to take a look at the cost of *not* risking their dreams: re-

gret, loss of self-esteem, and never knowing the excitement of living by faith.

*"What obstacles can you anticipate and how will you over-
come them?"* The most common obstacles are no time, no
money, no skill, and no helpers. However, none of these
need stop a dream. Skills can be learned from books or
from others and perfected by practice. Other people with
similar needs or vision can be recruited to share in the
dream. Often dreams can be funded from a variety of
sources, or less expensive alternatives can be found. And
time—well, we all have the same twenty-four hours a day.

Lynn was a twenty-seven-year-old, divorced mother
with custody of two sons, ages five and seven. She worked
as a clerk earning four hundred fifty dollars a month and
had earned seven college credits. During the next ten years
she was promoted up the career ladder to a well-paying
administrator position. She earned a doctorate degree,
wrote twenty books, joined the lecture circuit, and still
spent most evenings at home with her sons, until they became old enough to want to be with their friends some
evenings. How did she do it? Using the same twenty-four
hours a day that we all have, she learned housekeeping
shortcuts, gave up a few hours of sleep each night, said no
to demands on her time that did not relate directly to her
goals, and maximized every waking minute.

"Who can you recruit to be your team members?" We need
a caring group of friends and helpers who are committed
enough to the dream and to our friendship to give us honest feedback when we get off course.

*A team can be described as an interdependent group of people
working closely together toward a common goal, with agreed on
member responsibilities and standards.*

Interdependent: Team members need to recognize that
   they are dependent on one another to reach the

dream. A team is not just a collection of people with individual roles and responsibilities.

Working closely together: A team meets regularly to share, learn, plan, and evaluate.

Toward a common goal: The team must agree on the overall objectives of the dream. If some are striving for a perfect program and others are trying to gain personal recognition while still others are working at ministering to people, the dream will probably fail.

Agreeing on member responsibilities: Each team member must have responsibilities for a portion of the dream and must agree to fulfill those responsibilities. Nothing can destroy a dream more quickly than members who do not contribute to the dream and who are not there when they are needed.

And standards: Each team has standards for its members. These are the policies, procedures, rules, and lifestyles that members are expected to follow. All team members acknowledge that these norms are established to ensure that the ministry is successful.

"How will you handle the setbacks?" Just because there is a strong vision and a good dream does not mean that there won't be setbacks, disappointment, and discouragement. There will be. It is inevitable. You will want to help people think of the potential problems and develop a backup plan for coping. They should list whom they will call if they need extra help, whom to call in case of an emergency, and what to do at each step if part of the plan falls apart. Being prepared is the first step in coping with harsh realities.

"What do you need?" This question moves the process to the next step, where you facilitate the dream by mobilizing available resources.

Equipping the Team

"Sometimes a leader is like a coach for the team, sometimes like a team member, and sometimes like an equipment manager," one pastor suggests.

That's true. Good leaders function as coaches, contributing their own ideas to the brainstorming sessions, giving appropriate information, and providing training as needed. Training can be done by lecture, written materials, demonstration, observation, assisting, trying, and practicing. Leaders must explain what the limits are, if any. What is nonnegotiable? Some church policies and procedures are nonnegotiable and must be followed. Others can be changed through the proper channels. Some restrictions may be placed on the dream and these need to be stated up front.

One pastor whose church had a successful, smoothly operating monthly businessperson seminar discovered, almost by accident, that the guest speaker for the next month was a proponent of the new age movement. He quickly called the seminar team together and reiterated the nonnegotiable stipulation, "We will be distinctly Christian or we won't do these seminars. Our ministries will be biblically grounded."

In the role of coaches, leaders provide insight: "Here's how I envision the outcome of your present course of action." Leaders provide honesty. It's human to have mixed motives, but true leaders are honest about them and point out the truth to the team.

Leaders can also function as team members when they participate in developing a plan or strategy, in defining the goal, and in contributing personal knowledge and experience as well as information about the experiences of others. But these contributions are not to carry exaggerated weight. They are no less and no more valuable than the contributions of other team members. Sometimes leaders have to step in when things are not going smoothly and help out—not as leaders but as working team members.

Leaders function as equipment managers when they link people with other people who can add to the team; also when they find other resources such as money, equipment, space, literature, organizations (such as community agencies and nonprofit organizations that could assist in meeting the goals), and transportation. This is not to say that the leader has to be responsible for providing all of these things, just that most leaders have either the knowledge of or the access to these resources. By serving as a resource coordinator, the leader moves from the master to the servant role and begins to facilitate the people's dreams in the process.

Leaders also function as cheerleaders. They provide affirmation, encouragement, and lots of praise. Leaders are sure to give the credit for successful dreams to those whose dreams they were.

Empowering the Team

The power to effect the dream comes from the Holy Spirit, who is working within each believer. The Holy Spirit is all powerful and can bring to pass the most impossible of dreams if we are yielded to him.

When we as leaders step out of the way and release people to minister in the power of the Holy Spirit, we are, in effect, aiding in the empowering of the team. When we insist on maintaining total control of the dreams, the plans, the activities, and the decisions, we may be restricting the work of the Holy Spirit in the lives of our people.

There are three ways we can affirm that people are empowered.

1. Give the team decision-making authority and let people know that you have. When people come to you for information or decisions, direct them to the team.

2. Stand behind the team when it is under attack. When the dream begins to falter and a few things go wrong, there are always those ready to criticize. You can underscore the power of the team by standing by it.

3. Believe in the team. There is little that is more empowering than having faith in someone. When someone believes you can do something, you usually can! Empower your team by believing in it.

In your role as a leader you may find that one or more of these four areas need some work. Start today perfecting your skills in identifying needs, envisioning dreams, equipping your teams, and empowering your teams.

Product

Are We There Yet?

hen the product of management is task completion, success is easily measured. However, the product of leadership is developing people, so the results are sometimes more difficult to measure because progress is often slow. Since there are always more people to develop, we are never finished, we never "arrive" until our lives are over.

The challenge of developing people is exciting. Each day we get to ask anew, "Whom is God putting in my life today and what role am I to play in their lives?"

Ken was leading a men's group when he noticed a person who impressed him with a natural creativity, wisdom, and willingness to get involved. One day Ken asked him why he had never involved himself in the leadership of the group. The man replied that the former leader had told him that he was a good worker but wasn't leadership material. Ken shook his head in dismay. "That's not true," he insisted. "I think you'd be a terrific leader." Within a few months the man was a team leader and well on his way to realizing some of his dreams for ministry. He sent a card with a picture of a turtle on it to Ken. The card read, "Thanks for bringing me out of my shell." This is a result of leadership.

Leadership requires accepting people as they are, with strengths and weaknesses, gifts and eccentricities. When we commit ourselves to their development and resist the urge to panic over their defeats, real growth becomes possible. Too often leaders instill in people the feeling that they are inadequate or ill equipped for the tasks. Instead we need to recognize and draw out the creative resources that may be dormant within our people.

After two church experiences that were less than inspiring, Phil was beginning to think that perhaps he did not have whatever it took to be a minister. He had begun to believe that he was not very good at fitting in or pleasing people and that he was not naturally a very loving or kind person. He began to wonder if there would be a place for him in the Christian ministry at all. While interviewing to serve at the First Christ Church, he was torn between being brutally honest (and not getting hired) or making a good impression, giving the "correct" answers, and being untrue to who he really was. He chose to be honest whatever the consequences and answered their questions truthfully.

Phil had been told by leaders and had been convinced over the years that he had a rebellious attitude, was probably not a team player, and needed to become a different kind of person before God could use him in the ministry. Imagine his surprise when the staff and leaders of the church were unimpressed with his perceived failures.

What they wanted was an authentic person who could share both the ups and downs of life. They didn't want someone who "acted" like a pastor, they wanted a real person who happened to pastor. Phil now had no reason to hide, for even his idiosyncrasies were fodder for ministry. The church demonstrated leadership to him.

Here's another example of good leadership. "I hate missions!" Paul announced with his usual sensitivity and grace. Toshio, the missions director, never flinched as he asked Paul what it was about missions that Paul found so distasteful. In the minutes that followed, Paul shared his experience as a child whose parents served on the mission field. He described the hurt, frustration, and resentment he felt over the attitudes and behaviors he had witnessed growing up.

Toshio listened to him, then challenged him to develop a whole new way to look at missions that would help him break away from the pith-helmet stereotypes, remove the guilt from giving, and restore fun and adventure to this expression of the Christian life. As a result of this challenge Paul was confronted with the opportunity to do something to counter his frustration. He could continue to complain or he could help make a difference.

Out of his struggle emerged a plan to take groups of people on mission vacations for two-week periods. They visited exotic places, served the Lord, experienced cross-cultural relationships, and had fun vacations as well. Suddenly missions felt normal and personal. This was the product of patient leadership turning frustration into dreams of renewed ministry.

Patti loved to sing and dreamed of someday singing for the congregation. Her voice was clear but she sang softly and was passed over for choir and special music groups. She began to think her dream would never be realized. A new music director came to the church and heard of Patti's dream. He teamed her up with two other people whose voices blended. Then he worked with the sound engineer to secure the best microphones available and scheduled the group to give concerts throughout the area. With growing confidence their voices became stronger. Leadership must sometimes seek out the support that will enable people to serve with strength and confidence.

Bob was attending an annual pastor's conference for the first time. He was prepared to feel left out, insignificant, and awkward. The first day, three other pastors, who had attended together for years, spotted Bob as a newcomer and drew him into their circle. They ate meals with him, invited him to swim in the pool with them during free time, and included him in the after-hours pizza party. He left the conference feeling included, affirmed, inspired, and refreshed. A product of leadership.

Reaching Out

To whom do leaders reach out? It is easiest to reach out to those we identify as rising stars, to the people whom we immediately are drawn toward out of some personal preference. Sometimes God would prefer us to give a hand to the flickering candle that seems almost ready to go out. We may not see the potential in many of the people God brings to us, but as 1 Samuel 16:7 says, "The LORD does not look at the things man looks at. Man looks at the outward appearance, but the LORD looks at the heart." We must be willing to take a chance, to risk even our own reputations if need be, and reach out to whomever God gives us as dreamers of dreams and leaders of others.

Sometimes the people whom we are encouraging to develop new skills will embarrass us when they say or do something we think is inappropriate. Perhaps Jesus was embarrassed at times by the actions of those he had chosen as disciples or friends.

Was he embarrassed when . . .

- his mother pushed him into the limelight at the wedding at Cana?
- his mother and brothers came to where he was teaching and demanded that he come home with them?
- the mother of James and John tried to negotiate for a privileged place for her two sons?
- his followers criticized him for going home with Zacchaeus the despised tax collector?
- Peter cut off the ear of the servant of the high priest in the Garden of Gethsemane?
- the disciples argued with him trying to dissuade him from going into Jerusalem in the face of persecution?
- Mary and Martha squabbled over who did the most important work?

If we only reach out to develop those whom we know won't embarrass us, then we will miss many opportunities for leadership. In truth, each embarrassment and each failure can be a learning experience. Failure is not the end product unless we allow it to stop us from risking again. Surely when Jesus sent out the disciples two by two, he knew that some of them would ultimately tarnish his reputation. Yet he sent them out anyway. He didn't give them a ministry handbook or an emergency phone number so they could call him when they got into trouble. He didn't have them take an assortment of supplies, just in case, as we might have done. Instead, he "unpacked their bags," telling them what *not* to take: even apparent essentials like extra clothes, money, or provisions.

When we release people to ministry, we must remove the safety nets and give them freedom to fail. Only when we do that have we given them the freedom to succeed. We must be prepared for some surprises. People who are free may seem uncontrollable and things may become messy or seem unorganized according to our perception.

Coping with Discouragement

It is discouraging to invest in people and see them not making progress. Sometimes we begin to wonder if some people are worth the time and effort. Those feelings usually come when we forget that changing people is not *our* job but that of the Holy Spirit. Our responsibility is to lead, allowing God to work through us, enabling growth in others.

Our success lies in whether or not we are spending our time helping people identify needs and envision dreams and in equipping and empowering them to realize their dreams. If we are doing that, we can be assured that people will be growing, developing new skills, and ministering to others.

When discouragement comes, it may be helpful to consider the following questions.

- What expectations did I have that were unfulfilled?
- Who promised those expectations would be met?
- Were those expectations reasonable given what I know now?
- Have I been spending most of my time working, reacting, or managing instead of leading?
- How can I spend more time leading?
- If I were leading more effectively, what would I be doing differently?
- In what ways can I regroup and get the derailed dream back on track?

- With whom do I need to talk to regain my perspective?
- Have I been taking care of my own needs and dreams?
- How long do I need to feel discouraged?

Sometimes we find that we are the people God is developing as we act as leaders to others. Even in our discouragement we can begin to learn how to be more authentic, willing to risk and change, for the sake of God's kingdom.

Part 2

Redefining
the
Task

Management

Is It a Goal or a Tool?

I'm confused," Andre admits. "I've studied management skills and have tried to be both efficient and
effective as a minister, maximizing my time to do as
much ministry as I can. What's wrong with that?"
We're not saying that there isn't a place for managing
in the ministerial role, just that it must be a tool and not
the goal itself. When ministries are small or just beginning, the need for management is obvious. But as more
people get involved, there is an increased opportunity for
leadership.

Management versus Leadership

The following chart is a comparison of the differences between management and leadership. At first glance it might
appear that we are saying that management is all bad. Not
true. Managerial skills are essential if we are to get the job

done. However, we must see management as a tool to assist us in the task of leadership. Tools are immensely helpful. Attempting to dig a ditch or build a home without tools would be a waste of valuable time and effort! Trying to minister without some use of schedules, systems, procedures, and checks and balances would be foolish also.

Management	Leadership
• gets tasks done through people	• releases people to pursue their dreams
• uses people as tools to get job done	• uses management as a tool to develop people
• knows the limits based on scarcity of resources	• knows no limits believing that resources are unlimited
• solves problems	• enables people (and God) to solve problems
• plans, organizes, directs, controls, and evaluates to accomplish set tasks	• identifies needs, envisions dreams, equips, and empowers people to realize their dreams
• priorities are schedules, paperwork, procedures, chain of command, and allocation of resources	• priorities are people, dreams, ministry, affirmation, and trust in and obedience to the Lord
• authority comes from position, from God, and from personality	• authority comes from relationships, from God, and from personality
• focuses on efficiency, making things run smoothly, and doing things right	• focuses on effectiveness, ministering to people, and doing right things

Management	Leadership
• encourages dependence on manager for increased control	• encourages networking among the people for increased creativity
• business meetings are formal	• business meetings are more informal
• much of the work is done by designated leaders	• much of the work is done by members and newly emerging leaders
• creativity is limited	• creativity is encouraged
• communication is fairly formal	• communication is free flowing
• there are lots of layers in the organization	• there is a minimum number of layers in the organization

James D. Anderson and Ezra Earl Jones suggest a good model for ministry that illustrates three components: association leadership, organizational management, and spiritual direction.[1]

In this model the managerial approach is kept for the things that facilitate the realization of dreams and the outreach of ministry. Someone does have to be in charge of the budget and there must be some agreed on procedures for accountability and expenditure of funds. Someone must be responsible for maintaining the facilities. However, even in this model there is the potential for overmanaging and depriving people of the opportunity to develop new skills, so we must be open to letting go if the opportunity arises.

How would you respond if a couple of your people came in and said they had an idea about letting a street family live in one of your classrooms in exchange for providing janitorial services for the church? Many of us might be skeptical, suspicious, and uninterested, quickly looking for excuses such as zoning regulations and local fire codes, instead of pursuing the opportunity. It's hard to let go of being in control. When people get creative, things get shaken out of their neat little rhythms and operations.

One of the roles of ministry is providing spiritual direction. It must be kept in mind, however, that not all of that role is necessarily filled by the pastor or staff members. People within the body who are released to minister will be channels of spiritual direction from the Holy Spirit. When we retain all of this role for ourselves, we set ourselves up as spiritual gurus to whom everyone must come and from whom everyone must get their spiritual nourishment. That is not only draining on us but also restricts God's work in our ministry. He can work through all of our people, not just through a designated pastor.

We would add to the model, in the associated leadership role, identifying needs, envisioning dreams, equipping and empowering people to realize their dreams, and small groups. Small groups are one way the body can develop intimacy, vulnerability, and accountability within itself. We need a place where we can risk being totally honest, totally human, and totally ourselves and know that we will not be rejected. On the other hand we need members of our small group to not condone wrong or destructive choices we may make, so we must be willing to be accountable to one another. In the process of sharing who we are and where we are struggling, we invest in one another's lives and develop a strong bond of intimacy. Membership in a small group is hard and requires a serious investment of self. Bruce Larson, the recognized founder of the small group movement in our churches, says, "Get out of a small group if you can survive without them. I'm in one because I need it to survive."

When the Management Role Is Exclusively Used

"I hate to even suggest anything to our church board," George confesses. "Their first response is always negative. They see any change as upsetting the smooth operation of the church."

That's true of a lot of churches. Also some ministers act as mule drivers, using heavy-handed techniques. What is needed is a firm but light touch, guiding people in the use of their skills.

When a minister (lay or staff) overemphasizes the management role, several problems may exist or develop in the ministry or in the area of ministry under this particular minister:

- New, creative ideas may never get implemented.
- Few things get done on a timely basis because all decisions are funneled through the minister.
- Dreams get bottled up and frustrated.
- The overabundance of established controls may actually serve to thwart God's purposes.
- There is little direct communication between the minister and the people.
- People feel powerless and at the mercy of policies and procedures.
- There are more written procedures than are actually necessary and several copies of everything are filed and cross-filed.

When the Leadership Role Is Exclusively Used

"Don is the nicest person you'd ever want to meet. He's always ready to chat with you and share intimately. He is encouraging, affirming, and loving. He's also frustrating because he never follows through. If we tell him we need a bus for taking a group of seniors on an outing, he says, 'Fine,' and then nothing more is done about it. He keeps saying he's going to give some training classes but so far he never has. He's always too busy with people to get things done," complains one church member about her minister.

If a minister (lay or staff) ignores the basic managerial tasks that are necessary, then there will be problems:

- People will be frustrated because they don't have what they need to implement their dreams.
- There may be sloppy fiscal accountability, which is generally unacceptable.
- The facilities may become unsuitable (too dirty, cold, hot, broken down, etc.).
- Too much time is wasted by each person trying to work out the same logistics (such as reserving a room, a bus, or requesting funds) over and over, when establishing a simple procedure could facilitate the process and help dreams to become realities.
- Members feel loved and appreciated but the subordinate leaders feel unsupported and cast adrift.

A leader who has ignored the management role will need to build an appropriate level of managerial functions into the ministry. It will be uncomfortable at first to start exercising control and setting up procedures. However, the results will soon make up for the discomfort as the leader becomes used to using tools to facilitate the process of enabling dreams to become realities.

If the minister simply cannot become comfortable with even a minimal level of managerial functions, one option is to assign someone to serve as an administrator. One must be careful, however, that such an administrator understands that the goal is to provide only as much management as is necessary to enable ministry.

In one church there was an active outreach to migrant camps during the summer. Dozens of teams of high schoolers and college kids would go out and conduct vacation Bible school for the children. After three years a retired executive joined the church and was given the responsibility of coordinating this ministry. Within two months he had established so many procedures, deadlines, guidelines, rules, and regulations that the volunteers were confused and unmotivated to continue in the ministry. That year, less than half of the numbers of teams went out as had in each of the previous three years.

Comparison of Problem Solving

The manager follows a straight, linear progression when solving problems; moving from the problem, to alternatives, to selection of the best alternative, to implementation and evaluation.

The leader, on the other hand, has a totally different approach to problem solving, with the key element being involving team members in the process.

Both approaches will solve problems but in the leadership approach the people have a vested interest in the solution they helped develop. The people also develop problem-solving skills of their own—one of the goals of leadership.

What Do I Do?

Each minister (lay or staff) must make a personal choice about which approach to primarily use in ministry, whether to be more of a manager or more of a leader. But the real issue is whether we use management as a tool for ministry or people as tools for management.

Myths

How Can It Seem So Right and Be So Wrong?

I t is important to stop every so often and test our assumptions for accuracy. Let's look at some myths that we may have cherished as truths from time to time in our leadership development.

Here are twenty myths of leadership.

1. If it's not broken, don't fix it.

It is easy to reject new ideas from people if the current system seems to be working well. Creativity disrupts the status quo and that can be disconcerting. However, the new way might provide opportunities that otherwise will be missed. Perhaps doing things a different way will provide more opportunities for participation by a broader range of people. Perhaps the new idea will jog us out of our familiar rut. Smooth sailing is not always right, nor is it necessarily our goal. Welcome disruption, don't be afraid to take a second look.

2. Change comes easily if everyone agrees with the change.

Even when there is general agreement by the participants, it is not always easy to effect change. In making changes we disrupt routines, habits, and power structures. Some people may become uncomfortable and even resentful. We often discover adverse effects we hadn't anticipated and will have to be ready to make a few last-minute adjustments. If we approach any change expecting no problems, we will set ourselves up for inevitable disappointment.

3. Conflict is always bad.

People are bound to disagree since we are not clones of one another. As leaders we need to be open to negative feedback and differences of opinion and we need to encourage that openness in others. When people disagree with us we are forced to re-examine our position and either stand firm with a renewed commitment or compromise. When dealt with in a straightforward manner, conflicts can be catalysts for change in ourselves and others. Conflict can be dealt with constructively when we resist the urge to personalize our disagreement. This can be a challenge. One way to do it is to list the issues of disagreement and then explore each issue. Focus the discussions on the impact each proposed solution would have on the ministry and people. Keep from using phrases like "I disagree," "my way," or "I feel." Instead ask "What about another way?" or "How might people feel if . . .?" In this way the issue or solution is the center of attention and not you versus someone else. Focusing on confronting issues rather than beating or belittling people frees us to reduce conflicts to a resolvable level.

4. If you can't do it right, don't do it at all.

Waiting until we have all the resources to make a dream come true usually means that it never will. A dream to help all of the unwed mothers in your city who have no family needn't wait until you have a fully equipped facility. Start by helping one person in your own church.

Often the enthusiasm engendered by starting to make a dream come true is contagious and as others catch the vision, more resources become available. Want to do big things? Start with the small ones first.

5. *There is not enough money.*

Money is always an excuse and never a reason. There seems to never be enough money for anything worthwhile. The problem is not lack of money but rather it is lack of big enough dreams for ministry. God has more than enough money to fund our dreams if we allow ourselves to discover his vision for our world. He can provide resources beyond our limited expectations.

Over lunch a successful businessman shared with the pastor his recent commitment to Christ. It was exciting to hear as his contagious enthusiasm tumbled out. As they were parting he shook the pastor's hand and said, "By the way, Karl, if you ever need money for a special ministry just let me know." Of course the pastor didn't call him, but he appreciated the offer that had been made.

A few weeks later, Karl received a check at the church for several thousand dollars, with a note saying, "This is for anything you want to use it for, have fun." Not sure what to use it for, Karl deposited it with the accounting office and waited for an appropriately grand project that needed funding. After one year the pastor still hadn't spent the money. His friend called and they went out to lunch again. "Did I offend you or embarrass you?" he asked. "Are you angry with me for sending that money last year?" Karl assured him that he was neither angry, embarrassed, or offended; in fact he was rather flattered that he was trusted with the stewardship of such a large sum.

"Then why haven't you spent it?" the man asked. The pastor told him that he was waiting until an appropriate ministry need surfaced. He didn't want to squander this gift and he wanted to make the right choice, thus he had not spent the money. The businessman's face fell. "I guess you didn't understand, that was meant to be fun money, there is always more, but when you don't spend it I can't give more to replenish the supply. That robs me of the joy of giving!"

We limit ourselves not by lack of money but by a limitation of our faith. There is enough money in the world for all of our dreams if we would resist the urge to block what God would do.

6. Unmet needs mean there is something wrong with the church.

Susan was very disappointed with her first visit to a new church. "That's the coldest church I've ever been in," she complained.

Maybe it was an unfriendly place but Susan has some responsibility for reaching out to people, introducing herself, and letting others know she is a friendly person.

Some churches may not have a full range of programs to meet all of the needs of all of the people. Meeting needs starts with people perceiving needs to be met, then envisioning a dream to fulfill the needs. A fresh strategy develops when the people sense the needs and feel a desire to make a difference.

Too often we see the unmet need and are content to complain and place blame rather than taking the positive step to discover our role in meeting that need. Unmet needs can be a signal flare to alert us of a possible new direction for involvement and ministry.

7. Experts know best.

Granted, people who have studied and researched a topic and who are skilled in a specific aspect of ministry may be able to do a job well. But that does not mean that nonexperts shouldn't be allowed to take an active part in the leading of ministry.

Nonexperts, unhampered by knowing how something "ought to be done," often come up with new and creative ideas. Nonexperts are often willing to work hard at making a dream come alive. Nonexperts don't consider even menial tasks as being beneath them as some experts do. Nonexperts can also be full of enthusiasm and excitement at being able to assist in birthing a dream. It has been said that the problem with medicine is the doctors, the problem with law is the lawyers, and the problem with ministry is the ministers.

8. *Leaders should solve all of the problems.*

People who are uncomfortable with problems often jump too quickly to resolve them without taking time to consider all of the possibilities. Good leaders have learned to let people wrestle with problems for a while until they come to a good solution.

Solving a problem too quickly or solving all of the problems for people stifles growth and creates unhealthy dependence on the leader, as in the case of the child who tried to solve the cocoon problem and "helped" the butterfly go free by tearing open the cocoon. The butterfly couldn't fly because its wings hadn't been strengthened by the struggle of breaking free from the cocoon. People whose problems are always solved by others never learn problem-solving skills.

9. *Leaders are always nice.*

Certainly we strive to treat people with respect and dignity, but leaders are not necessarily nice all of the time. There is a time for disappointment, sadness, frustration, anger, and confrontation. Leaders are human beings with a full range of emotions and responses to life's interactions. When a leader offends, forgiveness must be sought just as when anyone else offends. Above all, our leaders need to be real.

Trying too hard to be nice takes its toll. It also signals a need within the person to be liked and gain approval. Trying very hard to be a good pastor, Antoine was overtly nice to people all day long at work. Yet when he came home he was irritable, impatient, frustrated, and genuinely unpleasant to be around. The wise advice of a friend surprised him. He suggested that Antoine try being tough and direct with people at work, so that he would find the energy and strength to be more gracious and kind at home. He discovered that he had been spending so much time pleasing people in the church that he had nothing left to give at home. In time Antoine discovered the freedom of being the same at work and at home, not having to please or pretend to be nice but to simply be real.

10. Leaders must be good at everything.

How often are we afraid to admit that we can't do something just because we somehow believe that we as leaders must know how to do everything?

Some people speak well, others are excellent musicians, some can organize a major event without a hitch, a few can talk intimately with near strangers, some can share Christ effectively, and others can discover the truth in people. Even Paul says we each have been given specific spiritual gifts. We are not alike and are not expected to be able to do everything. We believe this is God's design to help us recognize that we need each other.

11. Leaders should have clear visions to communicate.

It is true that leaders will have some of their own visions that they will share with the people but the primary task of being a leader is to assist others in identifying and envisioning their own dreams. When the only dreams of ministry come from the leader, the number and scope of the dreams are limited. When more people are freed up to dream, the number and scope of dreams are automatically increased. If one person can envision twenty dreams, one hundred people can envision two thousand dreams! The opportunities for ministry, for reaching people, and for developing people are staggering.

12. Leaders belong on a pedestal.

Putting leaders on pedestals is a way to neutralize their impact on our lives. It also relieves them from having to relate to people on an authentic, one-to-one basis. Pedestal sitters are expected to be perfect, better than the rest of us, and then are "rewarded" by being permitted a few idiosyncrasies or differences. While it is occasionally ego boosting to have people look up to and admire us, living on a pedestal is uncomfortable because of the isolation. Leaders need to be accepted for who they are and joined in their own spiritual journey of development by those people who are willing to enter into accountable, vulnerable relationships.

13. Leadership has its privileges.

There are some people in leadership positions who believe that because they are leaders, they are entitled to special privileges and don't have to follow the rules. Leaders are not exempted from God's laws. Leaders bear special responsibility to act in obedience regardless of the internal or external power they appear to possess. As leaders we are given the responsibility of modeling Christian behavior and setting a good example for our people.

There is growing awareness of the corruptibility of power. Henry Kissinger reminded us all, "Power is an aphrodisiac." Leaders are not exempt from the same ethical and moral mandates that God intended to regulate all of life. To think we are above the law begins the undermining of our integrity.

14. People are generally lazy, negative, unmotivated, and unwilling to work.

People tend to live up to or down to our expectations of them. Self-fulfilling prophecies being what they are, we will probably find a lot of lazy, negative, unmotivated people who are unwilling to work, if that is our expectation of people in general. This works in part because if we expect others to behave in a certain way, we will act accordingly. We will do most of the work ourselves, carrying most of the responsibility, solving the problems, and delegating very little.

When treated this way, many people will respond by sitting back feeling that if we don't want or need their help, they won't offer it. In effect we encourage and reinforce unresponsiveness by our controlling behavior. In reality there are plenty of enthusiastic, eager, ambitious, and competent people waiting to be given an opportunity to serve in a meaningful way.

15. People are generally loving, trustworthy, helpful, and faithful.

Not necessarily so. While it is no doubt true that there are many people out there who embody all of these fine traits, it is important to remember the insight David Augsburger shared, "We live in a world of broken trust." People are going to let us down, break our confidences, misplace or damage our possessions, forget us, leave us out, and not live up to their commitments. We mustn't be surprised or devastated when this happens, as it surely will. Granting and receiving forgiveness are key to restoring broken relationships and moving on.

16. People will appreciate the leaders and tell them so.

Every so often one does get affirmed and appreciated as a leader but not nearly as often as one would like. It's nice to receive notes of appreciation, but more likely you will instead be reading "hate mail" and wondering if anyone cares. Even when we receive lots of affirmation and support, it is often the negative comments that stay foremost in our minds. Hopefully there are people in our lives who let us know we are loved, who provide affirmation and support. Bruce Larson reminds us that "it takes ten 'atta boys' to make up for one 'you jerk.'" We need an ongoing support group in our lives to help keep perspective. If you have a few people to let you know you are appreciated, it can make a world of difference.

17. The church is only an organization.

While the church is an organization, it is more. It is a living organism. When we consider the organic nature of the church as the body of Christ, the fundamental idea of a corporate personality with Christ emerges. As an organism that is alive through the Holy Spirit, the church assumes a personality shaped by her relationship with Christ. This personality cannot be achieved by human effort nor can it be regulated or controlled by people. It is, however, observable and recognizable to those within and without the bonds of fellowship. This personality is the result of faithful discipleship.

To say that the church is the body of Christ is to affirm the new identity we have as people who have been born again by faith, have died to the power of sin, and have been raised to new life in Christ. As followers of Jesus we grow out of individualism into fellowship, united in love with all who have been called to communion with Christ. As a body we are empowered to grow in love and serve with humble faithfulness as the risen Lord, our head, works in and through us.

The church, then, is by nature an organic entity capable of life and growth. It is created by Christ and exists because of the faithful response to his call by those who serve him. The church functions as the body of Christ in which individual members are joined together in fellowship with one another as well as in relationship with the Lord.

18. The church is only an organism.

Organization is not alien, nor is it destructive to an organism. There are organizational elements within organic systems that enable the organism to function according to its purpose.

It has been said that the church as the fellowship of believers is an organism but never an organization. Brunner writes, "As the body of Christ, the church has nothing to do with an organization and has nothing of the character of the institutional about it." However, it is our assertion that the nature of the church necessarily includes both organic and organizational dimensions. To eliminate either aspect results in an entity that is less than the true church.

We use the term *organization* to mean a group of persons who are united by choice to fulfill a purpose. As such, the church is an organization as well as a living organism.

19. The church should operate like a business or the military.

In business the product is goods or services. In the military the product is a fighting machine. In ministry the product is changed lives as people develop new skills, new relationships, and new ministries. While the pastor may consider him- or herself the chief executive officer (CEO) or the captain of the ship, in reality there is more to ministry than either of these titles imply.

The goals, strategies, and operational decision-making processes of the church differ significantly from those of business and military structures because priorities and premises are different.

20. The pastor is a shepherd.

Misuse of the biblical image of Jesus "shepherding the flock" has created great misunderstanding of the leadership roles in the church. The inordinate desire of many pastors to feel needed leads them to adopt this model of ministry to the extreme, where they see themselves as symbolic carriers of people, in the way shepherds haul sheep around in their arms.

Even if we could carry one or two sheep in our arms, we couldn't carry the whole flock. Also our hands would be unavailable for anything else. We sometimes act as shepherds in the sense that we provide some of the resources for the sheep, we provide some protection from dangers, and we guide and direct at times. But Jesus is still *the* shepherd of the flock.

Once we have identified some of our faulty assumptions, we must be willing to let go of them. It may take several conscious attempts before you can break the habit of believing a myth; however, keep at it, for new ways of thinking result in new ways of living.

Ten Commandments for Leaders

The following ten commandments are a variation of Intrapreneur's ten commandments developed by Gifford Pinchot III in *Intrapreneuring*.[1]

1. Be prepared to be fired every day.
2. Do not let procedures, policies, or people stop your dream.
3. Do not feel that any task is beneath you, but don't try to do everyone else's job either.
4. Draw a circle of people around you to be your team.
5. Trust God to know why he has brought certain people to you and work with them.
6. Don't seek publicity for your ministry for the sake of ego gratification.
7. Don't forget we live in a world of broken trust and there are no guarantees.
8. It is easier to ask forgiveness than permission. (Note: This may not be true in all situations.)
9. Don't ever forsake your God-given dream, but be willing to start small if necessary.
10. Treat everyone with dignity and respect.

Motivation

Where Does It Come From?

ourteen people came forward last spring at the end of our missions conference," one pastor shares. "They were committing their lives to full-time Christian service. To date thirteen have done nothing about that commitment. Only one has moved ahead. He quit his full-time job, applied to a missions board, and hopefully will be accepted for the field. But, it's so discouraging!"

It's a typical story. People may respond emotionally to a great speaker or a challenge but unless there is something more than a great speech or an exciting challenge, there is often no follow-through.

What makes the difference? Where does motivation come from?

Entrepreneur Jim Rohn tells the story of his early days in leadership. He had a little sales organization of five or six people. He was so excited by the financial opportunities and the incredible possibilities for the organization that he worked night and day. He told himself he was going to make his people successful if it killed him. "I almost died!" he confesses.

Frank Tillapaugh says that leaders cannot provide the same, lasting motivation that comes from within, that "I want to do it" determination. We can temporarily get people to do something through guilt, "you ought to do this," or by promising rewards, "God will bless you if you do that." But neither of these approaches produces lasting motivation.

Needs and Drives

That "I want to do it" motivation comes from a desire to meet some need within us. When we have a need, we experience a strong drive to achieve the goal of meeting that need.

Think of the need for food. When we are hungry we experience a drive to eat, after which we are satisfied. But when we are hungry again, the cycle starts all over.

There are many needs that drive people to ministry. Some are healthy, others are not. Wise leaders will get to know the people who are ministering with them and learn their motives. The problem is that almost any healthy need can become unhealthy if carried to an extreme. For example, a normal need to be recognized can become an unhealthy need to be the center of attention. People with strong needs will be some of our best leaders but they may need judicious feedback to prevent them from allowing their own needs to dominate their ministry.

What are some of the needs that drive people to ministry?

Need to Be Loved

Shanelle needs to be loved, so she reaches out in love to everyone around her. She is a greeter at the Sunday morning service and most people feel a little better just seeing her smile and shaking her hand. She really cares about people. This is healthy.

Paula desperately needs to be loved. An abused child and a battered wife, she has lacked love most of her life. Paula goes out of her way to do things for people to the point of being a nuisance. Often during fellowship time, she interrupts serious conversations to offer cookies, coffee, punch, or peanuts and she persists, almost to the point of arguing, when someone refuses her offer. This is unhealthy.

Need to Be Recognized

Nathan has a need to be recognized. He works as a sound guy for one of the singing groups at church. He enjoys seeing his name on the back of the program. He keeps copies in his scrapbook. Healthy.

Mark has a tremendous need to be recognized. He is forever donating things to the church ever since they put a little plaque on the potted palm he donated. He provides pens for the pastors that say "donated by Mark H_____," and he wants his name listed in the bulletin for every donation. Unhealthy.

Need to Be Understood

Donna has a need to be understood. She will take the time to discuss her ideas, share her opinions, and risk being open and vulnerable with others on the team. She is very articulate. Healthy.

Yoko has an overwhelming need to be understood. Long after a decision has been made, she is still going around to team members trying to explain or re-explain her point of view (whether or not hers was the one adopted by the team). She will debate an unimportant point, dragging in facts, figures, and examples. She is relentless. Unhealthy.

Need to Achieve

Diego has a need to achieve. He is very goal oriented, so when he chooses a ministry, he writes down the expectations, develops a plan to reach the objectives, and begins implementing the plan. He always follows through. Healthy.

Larry has an exaggerated need to achieve. He wants to win at all costs. He is often reckless and even ruthless in his determination to do the best and have the best ministry. He considers the slightest setback a total failure and thinks he must then redouble his striving efforts. If necessary, Larry will work eighteen to twenty hours a day. Unhealthy.

Need to Know

Vera has a need to know. So she studies, she reads, and she listens. She is very helpful as a team member because she can usually answer questions such as, "How do we go about getting a parade permit?" What she doesn't know, she loves to research and find out. Healthy.

Tammy has an immense need to know all about everything and everybody. She is nosy and pushes her way into obviously private conversations. She reads personal files and other people's notes and loves to listen to gossip. If something is brought up at a team meeting that she has not yet heard about, she is livid because she believes people were deliberately sneaking behind her back and leaving her out. Unhealthy.

Need for Responsibility

Jerry has a need for responsibility. He willingly accepts jobs assigned him in team meetings and carries them out with predictable competence and reliability. Healthy.

Oscar has an oversized need for responsibility. He volunteers for everything and is upset if a new task is assigned to anyone else. He doesn't always fulfill his responsibilities but he figures that neglecting one out of four or five isn't too bad considering those he does fulfill. Unhealthy.

Need to Belong

Ellen has a need to belong. She is a member of a small support group at church, has three very close friends, and serves as a team member on two ministry project teams. Healthy.

Jasmine has an insatiable need to belong. She believes she must be a member of every ministry project team, committee, task group, special prayer chain, women's committee, and board. When she isn't included in something she is devastated and sinks into a depression, feeling totally rejected. Unhealthy.

Need for Security

Aaron has a need for security. He is the cautious member of the budget committee who carefully weighs financial opportunities or requests before giving his recommendation or vote. He is the one who always encourages the team to take a second look to see if they've overlooked something. Healthy.

Bill has an excessive need for security. No change is ever good to him. He is comfortable with things the way they are and never sees a need for change. If changes are adopted, Bill becomes apprehensive, fearful, and stressed out. Unhealthy.

Need for Excitement

Annika has a need for excitement. She is always ready to try something new and take on a different ministry and she enjoys the thrill of new risks. Her enthusiasm is contagious and she is a fun member of the team. Healthy.

Cherise has an insatiable need for excitement. She never wants to do anything the same way twice. Everything must be done differently, every time! She is a risk taker and rarely stops to plan, count the cost, or even consider normal safety precautions. Unhealthy.

Need for a Clear Conscience

Miguel has a need for a clear conscience. He gladly makes himself open, with vulnerability and accountability, to his small support group and the team members with whom he works. Miguel's integrity is beyond question and the decisions he makes are based on "What would God want me to do in this situation?" Healthy.

Everett has an inordinate need for a clear conscience. He confesses every wrong thought or deed to everyone he talks with, often inappropriately. He asks forgiveness at the drop of a hat, warranted or not. Decisions are difficult for him to make because he's afraid he is wrong or will be misunderstood. He goes out of his way to interrupt team proceedings to ensure that everyone is pleased with him. Unhealthy.

Need for Closure

Sherrie has a need for closure. She is a good facilitator at team meetings because she keeps track of decisions made and ensures that responsibilities are assigned and agreed to. At the end of the meetings someone on the team usually turns to Sherrie and asks, "Have we left anything open?" knowing that she will have kept track. Healthy.

Ila has an urgent need for closure. She cannot stand having an open discussion where people move from one idea to another. She stifles creativity by insisting that "we finish this issue before going on to the next!" Unhealthy.

Need for Freedom

Chris has a need for freedom. He enjoys operating in a very loose environment where his creativity can flow freely. Other people like to take his ideas and give them structure and reality. Chris doesn't mind, as long as he is free to come up with new ideas and approaches to ministry. Healthy.

Derrick has a need for total freedom. He doesn't want to be told what to do or when to do it. He doesn't pay attention to the schedule and usually misses team meetings. He doesn't submit reports or follow through on commitments because he "isn't in the mood." Unhealthy.

Temptations to Avoid

Here are a few temptations to avoid in the area of motivation.

Manipulation

It would be easy to watch individuals, determine what their primary driving needs are, and then use a need to get them to do what we want them to do. If Kyle is a person who desperately needs to be recognized, he could easily be influenced to tackle a new project or give a generous donation if he were promised a bronze plaque with his name on it displayed prominently in the church. Giving a plaque for recognition is fine. Using a need for recognition to force someone into ministry is not.

Using Needy People for Everything

Sometimes it is nice to have needy people as members of your team. They will work around the clock for love and attention or to achieve, to obtain closure, or to assume more responsibility. That's fine as long as their needs are on a healthy level. However, if all of your team members are compensating for need levels in unhealthy ways, then you as a leader will want to work less on the programs and more on the people so they can learn to meet their needs at a healthy level. Watch the workaholics. Thank them and send them home early. Give them love, attention, and recognition *before* they finish the project.

Seeing People as Mules

Harry Levinson writes about the motivational theory of the carrot and the stick.[1] He asks us to picture the carrot and the stick routine in which the central figure is a stubborn mule. When we adopt the reward and punishment theory we are thinking of people as mules to be manipulated and controlled. If we think of people this way, we are placing ourselves in a superior, condescending position. The results in the ministry are inefficiency, lower productivity, less commitment, fewer dreams, and almost no creativity from people.

The reward and punishment theory stems from what Douglas McGregor calls Theory X Assumptions about people.[2] These assumptions are: that people basically dislike work and will avoid it if possible; that people must be coerced into productivity; and that people prefer to be directed and resist responsibility.

This is not necessarily true. McGregor's Theory Y Assumptions make more sense in ministry. They are: that work is as natural as play; that people will work willingly toward a goal they are committed to; that people seek responsibility; that people are basically creative; and that people have a great deal of untapped personal potential.

Motivational Roles

There are several tasks in the motivational process and only some of them belong to the leader. The other roles belong to the Holy Spirit and the individual as outlined in the chart below.

When we as leaders try to take on parts of the other roles, we are unable to fulfill our own role of being the facilitator of ministry and we develop a following of dependent people.

Holy Spirit (provides impetus)	Individual (provides will)	Leader (provides support)
• Makes individual aware of need	• Experiences need	• Acknowledges need
• Gives individual the vision, the dream, the ideas	• Experiences vision, ideas, and dreams	• Listens to and affirms the ideas, dreams, and visions

Holy Spirit (provides impetus)	Individual (provides will)	Leader (provides support)
		• Provides opportunities for ministry
• Gives spiritual gifts and natural abilities to individual	• Has spiritual gifts and natural abilities	• Recognizes and affirms spiritual gifts and natural abilities
	• Develops goals	• Asks questions of individual to help develop or clarify goals
• Inspires the individual with desire to minister	• Chooses to commit to the ministry goal	• Encourages the commitment
• Gives enthusiasm	• Is willing, excited	• Affirms progress
		• Provides resources
• Provides guidance	• Is obedient	• Is supportive
• Provides strength	• Persists against all odds	• Removes obstacles
• Is faithful	• Completes task	• Celebrates and recognizes the achievement

What Leaders Can Do

While we cannot motivate people ourselves, we can facilitate the process of motivation. Frederick Herzberg found that people are likely to be motivated in an organization where the work is important and where there is an opportunity for achievement, recognition, responsibility, and advancement. Things such as policies, administration, supervision, working conditions, salary, and interpersonal relationships make people unhappy and dissatisfied if they aren't acceptable but they don't necessarily affect the motivation level of the people.

Knowing this, we as leaders can focus our energies on letting people discover the importance of the ministry and then get out of the way and let the people assume responsibility and achieve their dreams. Our role is to provide support, affirmation, encouragement, and recognition.

There are key stages in a ministry that are particularly motivating and inspiring.

Dreaming

Just sitting together and dreaming the big dream can be exciting. When we invite people to share their dreams we unleash within them that inner excitement that motivates them.

Deciding

After dreaming comes a moment when the decision is made to do something. The indecision is over. We are committed and it feels terrific. When our people decide to commit to a dream, we must cheer them on and help them unleash the determination within that will motivate them.

Planning

As we develop concrete plans, the dream takes on shape and strength. Our commitment and faith increase as we envision what the dream will look like. Encourage people to plan thoroughly and then to unleash the curiosity within them to see the plan develop into a reality. The curiosity will drive creativity and encourage commitment to the plan.

Starting

There is a great sense of accomplishment in actually starting something. Remember that first day of a new diet? Hungry yes but feeling great! Be there when your people start a new ministry. Affirm and encourage them. Celebrate their excitement and motivation.

Progressing

Some projects take so long to complete that achievement of interim steps needs to be celebrated to maintain enthusiasm. Watch for growth and development, then affirm the person to boost his or her self-esteem.

Completing

What a thrill to complete a project or get a new ministry organized and launched. Don't miss out on the celebration. Cultivate the joy in your people that will motivate them to more growth and more ministry.

What Wise Leaders Don't Do

We may not be able to motivate people at will but we can definitely unmotivate them! Here are some things wise leaders will want to avoid:

- being unavailable to people
- belittling people or their dreams

- responding negatively to dreams
- insisting on our own dreams
- not providing resources
- discouraging creativity
- putting too many restrictions on dreams
- making the paperwork too complicated and time consuming
- having too many levels of review
- never complimenting people
- not recognizing achievement
- taking all the credit for success
- blaming people for failures
- keeping information to ourself

Take a few minutes to consider what role you have been playing in the motivational process of your people. Are you a facilitator or a frustrator of dreams?

8

Manipulation

Why Can't I Have It My Way?

And then we sang at Disneyland," the choral director concluded his glowing report of the group's tour, as he spoke one Sunday evening at church.

It made a great story, but the sixteen group members were a little shocked. It was technically true. While on a half-day free-time excursion to Disneyland, they had playfully sung a few bars of a chorus as they waited in line for one of the rides. They had sung at Disneyland. But the director was implying that they had performed there, which wasn't true.

We are all tempted, at times, to manipulate our worlds, to color the truth, in order to put ourselves in a better light or to simply get our way. But manipulation is wrong. The dictionary says that manipulation is to influence craftily, to handle skillfully, or to alter to suit our own purposes. Paul says in 2 Corinthians 4:1–2, "Therefore, since through God's mercy we have this ministry, we do not lose heart.

Rather, we have renounced secret and shameful ways; we do not use deception, nor do we distort the word of God. On the contrary, by setting forth the truth plainly we commend ourselves to every man's conscience in the sight of God."

When we distort the facts, exaggerate the numbers, or misuse resources (time, money, or attention) to coerce the world into believing what we want it to or acting as we want it to, we are acting craftily and often dishonestly.

Temptations to Manipulate

It's tempting sometimes to manipulate our worlds because it is often easy to do. Here are a few of the more common traps.

Manipulating the Numbers

Don't say there were ten hands raised for salvation at the end of a service when there were only two. Don't claim there were one hundred at the Easter sunrise service when there were twenty-five. In a world where advertisers have made us believe that everything must be bigger and better and that more is best, we may find ourselves exaggerating the numbers. But remember that to God, one person would have been enough to warrant sending his Son. If one soul is all that responds, that should be enough for us.

Manipulating the Truth

At a citywide youth rally a pastor had asked several high schoolers to give their testimonies. One was involved in sports and shared how God helped him to be a witness on the team. One girl told how she depended on God to help her resist the temptation of premarital sex. When the third kid stood up, the pastor (wanting to reach teenagers who were involved with drugs) introduced the young man, saying that God had saved him from a life of drugs. The boy, not knowing what else to do, gave a glowing (and untrue) testimony about being cured from using drugs. Effective but wrong.

It was true that but for the grace of God that young man could have been on drugs, and it was true that God had given him a strong Christian family and had "saved" him from getting involved with drugs. But even if the pastor didn't actually tell a lie, he certainly manipulated the audience into believing a lie and the young man into telling one.

When we manipulate the truth, we are saying that we don't believe that the truth is enough. If we believe that what is isn't what is needed, we ought to be out changing what is, not changing what we say about what is.

Manipulating People

There are many ways we manipulate people every day of our lives. We each influence other people, whether we are conscious of it or not. How we use that influence is important. The real issues are attitude and intent. If we can influence people to follow the Lord by our example, if we can inspire people to make positive life changes by our message, we have executed influence. But we have not tried to craftily manipulate them for our own selfish purposes. That is the difference. Let's look at a few types of manipulation common in leadership.

Bonnie-the-Bean-Counter

Bonnie works in the accounting office at a large church. Her job is to be sure that every voucher, every invoice, and every order form matches, and to ensure that every form is completed perfectly and promptly. If a request for a check is not submitted exactly fifteen working days before the check is needed (per the written policy), the check will not be ready on time. If 9:00 A.M. is the cutoff, 9:05 A.M. is too late.

Bonnie sent a nasty letter to one of the pastors because he had not noted the city for two of his telephone calls in his weekly long-distance telephone log. Her assumption was that he had deliberately neglected to do so out of a blatant and rebellious disregard for the procedure. The truth was that he had simply returned a couple of phone messages and hadn't known the city he was calling.

Bean counters are people who focus on the systems, procedures, policies, and minutia to the point of missing the message. They end up hampering the ministry. Their basic issue is absolute control of everything within their responsibility and of the people with whom they come into contact.

There was a large church that had a nice reception room on the second floor, which was often used for wedding receptions. There were several round tables in an adjacent storage room, which were available if the party wanted to use them. When a group wanted to have a luncheon downstairs in another room they were told by a bean counter they would have to rent tables because the round tables were to be used upstairs only!

There are bean counters everywhere. In small churches they will effectively stunt the growth of the church. In large churches they will tend to stifle only portions of the ministry. Bean counters need to learn to eliminate unnecessary controls and trust people, believing that they are honest and cooperative most of the time.

The apostle Paul talks about a form of bean counting when he discusses how some people focus on the strict dietary laws given in the Old Testament. Even though this passage refers to whether or not to eat meat, the principle is the same. He says "therefore let us stop passing judgment on one another. Instead, make up your mind not to put any stumbling block or obstacle in your brother's way. . . . Let us therefore make every effort to do what leads to peace and to mutual edification. Do not destroy the work of God for the sake of food" (Rom. 14:13, 19–20).

We must learn not to focus on the minutia but the ministry.

Tom-the-Tyrant

Tom is a senior pastor who believes that he has "The Vision" for the church and tolerates no differences of opinion. He sets the policy, outlines the procedures, makes the rules, and deals harshly with anyone who doesn't fall into line. When Tom came to his church, he, like other tyrants, fired all of the existing staff and brought in his own people. He basically rules by fear and intimidation. Staff have learned not to make creative suggestions because anything Tom doesn't like, he holds up to public ridicule.

Tyrants are always ready to expand their sphere of influence. They start with one church, then a satellite church, then a school, a television program, and who knows what else! Tyrants are effective at doing big projects and at controlling people but are not often that effective in the daily walk of relating to one another as members of the body of Christ.

Tyrants can be stopped in a church if the people rise up in a unified protest, but when tyrants feel their power slipping, instead of changing themselves, they usually change churches. Peter says to leaders, "Don't be tyrants, but lead them by your good example . . ." (1 Peter 5:2 TLB).

Patti-the-People-Pleaser

Patti will do almost anything to please people, which can be a subtle form of manipulation. People pleasers keep others happy by finding out what they want and giving it to them. Patti is a democrat with democrats and a republican with republicans. She loves the Sunday school curriculum when talking to the teacher and hates it when listening to the student complaining. Patti plans ways to please people that sometimes forces them to go along with her ideas rather than do what they would like.

Recently Patti volunteered to be in charge of the food for a Sunday school class picnic. She planned an elaborate spread and spent the entire morning getting everything ready. She grilled hamburgers and was ready to serve promptly at 12:00 noon. Unfortunately a softball game was in progress at that time and the score was tied. None of the players or spectators wanted to stop and eat but they did because Patti had gone to all that work. (True, but she might have checked with the class to see when would have been the best time to start the hamburgers.)

People pleasers use guilt to manipulate people, making them feel obligated to do what is wanted because of the sacrifices the pleasers have made. Unasked-for sacrifices!

Some people pleasers aren't aware that they are manipulating people. They simply feel such a need for love, acceptance, and approval that they will do anything to get it, including emotional blackmail.

People pleasers can break out of that syndrome with a conscious choice to do what is right, to be who they are, and to seek to please God first. Paul says "For am I now seeking the favor of men, or of God? Or am I striving to please men? If I were still trying to please men, I would not be a bond-servant of Christ" (Gal. 1:10 NASB).

Harry-the-Helpless

Harry never has to do anything and avoids all responsibility because poor Harry is helpless. Everyone knows it. Harry isn't asked to set up tables because he'll drop one on his foot (like last year) or set them wrong. Harry isn't asked to go to the printers to pick up the bulletins because he has no sense of direction and will get lost (twice last year). Harry doesn't teach a class because he can't stand up in front of a group, doesn't participate in a small group because he's shy, and doesn't lead the singing because he can't carry a tune. In fact Harry can't do anything!

Except for one thing. Harry is very good at manipulating everyone around him into doing things for him. All he has to do is demonstrate his helplessness. People who choose to be helpless get a lot of attention and even though some of it is negative attention ("Can't you ever do anything?"), they love it.

"Helpless" people have learned that they can exercise a lot of power by being passive. If things aren't the way they want them to be, they simply withhold approval or response or refuse to participate and things get changed.

Paul had no patience with those who wouldn't pull their share of the work. He said they shouldn't get to eat (2 Thess. 3:10–11). And Proverbs 18:9 says "He also who is slack in his work is a brother to him who destroys" (NASB). It is destructive to have team members who pretend helplessness or who refuse to develop any skills for the ministry.

Results of Manipulation

Anytime a leader gives in to the temptation to manipulate, the results are predictable. We lose credibility with people and our effectiveness is seriously reduced whenever we are found out. Even when we are telling the truth, we won't be believed, once people learn that we sometimes stretch the truth or change the facts. When people discover that we play games to manipulate them, they will be reluctant to trust us or to work toward a cooperative relationship with us in ministry. People will become suspicious of even our best motives and ideas. And those who feel used by our manipulations become angry, hurt, and resentful.

There are few positive benefits of manipulation and those are short lived, lasting only until we are found out!

Manipulation is competition gone wrong. It is not fair play, not being a good sport. Manipulation is like deliberately fouling an opponent in basketball as soon as the referee isn't looking.

Beyond Manipulation

There is a better way. Here are some steps.

Recognize the propensity to manipulate. We are all tempted sometimes to make things sound better than they are. We like getting our own way, so we are tempted from time to time to manipulate the facts, the truth, or people. Learn to recognize when it is that you are prone to consider manipulation and build in safeguards so that you can avoid these situations. Review periodically what you've said and how you've acted so that you can detect your tendency to manipulate. Ask people you trust to tell you how you are behaving or if they see you beginning to play games with people. This is hard because it means you will be vulnerable with people and you may not like what you hear.

Choose not to manipulate. Make a conscious decision that you will not be a manipulator, that you will not be crafty and cunning. Decide that you are committed to the leadership approach for the duration and don't let anything pull you off course, even if things appear to be falling apart. A person who is a true leader, working to develop strong people, will not manipulate people or situations. Begin "truth testing" your stories and statements in order to ensure that you are being open, honest, and loving in your relationships and in your ministry.

Recognize that you don't always have the *answer.* Even when you think that you have a better idea and know how things should be done, keep in mind that there might be several good ideas and many ways to successfully minister in a given area. If we believe that people are generally competent and capable, then we can trust them to have viable dreams and ministries.

Live lovingly. If we see people with the eyes of love, if we act toward them in loving ways, if we always choose the loving alternative, we will not become manipulators. We will be fulfilling one of God's goals for us—right relationships with one another.

Part 3

Looking in the Mirror

Determination

Who Is in Control?

I used to have all of the decisions come through me," one leader confesses. "If I reviewed and approved or disapproved every activity, outreach, social, program, purchase, and outside speaker, I could control the ministry. But my desk was beginning to be the great lost and found department. Everything was 'lost' and 'found' there! I was a bottleneck. Finally, my staff convinced me to try trusting them a little and letting go of some of the decisions. So I did. Now, I don't make many of the decisions at all. In fact I'm not sure who's in control!"

Control is a major issue with most people in positions of leadership. Many people who gravitate toward leadership like things to be orderly, correct, and done on time. Most of them have creative ideas and a vision of how their particular ministry could look if it were done well. So it follows naturally that these people would have a tendency to want to control the ministry.

Why We Control

From the time we are young, we are taught to control ourselves and those around us. How often have you heard someone say the following?

"Why don't you control your children?"
"Control your temper!"
"Control yourself!"
"Don't lose control."
"Maintain self-control."

We are taught to control our movements. Adults don't flail around as babies do. We are taught to control our bodily functions and even apologize for such things as burps and stomach growls. Control is a major issue. Some control is, of course, good. We need to exercise self-control. We can't go around biting people or destroying things because we are angry. But excessive control is a problem, even when we are dealing with feelings. Suppressed negative feelings fester and keep us from wholesome and healthy relationships. Finding the desired balance of control is an important challenge.

There are other reasons we seek to rigidly control our environments in general and our ministries in particular.

We don't want to fail. "When I came to this church, I promised that we'd have a strong children's program. I've been here six months and it hasn't happened. Now, I have to step in and do it myself to make sure we accomplish my goal. Otherwise, I will not live up to my promise," Harry explains.

We are often content to relinquish control when our people are keeping dreams on track and things are going well. But when their best efforts don't seem to be work-

ing out, we usually step in and take back control to ensure against failure. We rescue. We protect our reputation
because when our people fail we believe that we have
failed. And we see failure as a terrible end to a dream.

However, failure needn't be the end! Failure is merely
a signal that the game plan needs to be changed, that adjustments must be made before we try again.

When we are tempted to take back control it is important for us to remember that our goal is not so much developing the program as it is developing people. Perhaps
our people need a little failure to teach them how to make
better plans, how to stay on track, how to reevaluate, how
to regroup, how to cope, and how to persist. Rescuing robs
them of the lesson.

Andy took the developing-people approach. To promote
a weekend conference she was planning, one of Andy's
lay leaders developed a terrifically clever brochure and
came to him for approval. Andy affirmed the cleverness
and the plans but suggested possible problems. The brochure,
for example, left off several important pieces of information and didn't clarify what the conference was all about.
Andy mentioned these things to the lay leader, who dis-
regarded everything and didn't change the brochure. The
conference lost three thousand dollars because registration was low. Later a lot of people told Andy they would
have come if they had understood what the conference
was about! Andy met with the lay leader after the conference and they debriefed the event. Because Andy was
nonjudgmental, the lay leader was free to admit that she
had learned a lesson and that next time she would know
better what to do. The program may have failed from a financial perspective, but Andy succeeded in developing his
lay leader.

We want it done our way. Maria was hosting a citywide
pastors' conference at her church. She personally took care
of every detail, from the luncheon menu and place cards

to copying and collating the handouts, to registration and evaluation. When asked if she needed help, she smilingly declined. "I want to make sure everything is exactly the way I want it to be," an exhausted Maria admitted privately to her friend.

Some of us are willing to release people as long as they stick to the plan and get the program on line! But when things aren't happening according to our own dreams or ideas, we take back the control and force things to go our way.

It may be fine for Maria to try to control all of the small responsibilities but what if she took the same approach with a large conference? It couldn't work. In order to have absolute control, we have to keep things fairly small. This means that our ministries and our dreams must remain small. If we are to experience the dreams God has given us, we must be willing to let people work out those dreams and let God be in control. Only then will the ministry grow.

We don't want people to find out our shortcomings. Ivan's story is typical. "When I'm in charge, I can direct things into areas where I am strong, so I look good to people. I know what's going on. I don't look foolish or inept."

A lot of leaders would sympathize. When we let people dream their own dreams, we sometimes have to admit our uncertainty when asked how to implement the dream or what the status of the dream is. It may be a bit disconcerting the first time a pastor has to say he doesn't know what time the leadership training is that night or how one goes about getting signed up for the weekend retreat. As long as we harbor the belief that a leader is one who knows it all, we will have difficulty letting go of the controls. However, it's not important that leaders know all the details, as long as they know to whom to refer inquiries.

One pastor used to insist that he do all the preaching and speaking for the church programs, with the exception of Sunday school classes. He didn't have a traditional home visitation night because he was uncomfortable making calls. Finally, one of his deacons gently counseled him. "You don't have to do everything! Let some of us do what we're good at! Some of us can teach, others can speak, and several of us like to do home visitations!" Right!

We are afraid of rejection. Joe is a very controlling pastor. His "team" is really just a collection of people who carry out his dreams, his way. Once, in a rare moment of self-disclosure, Joe confessed, "As long as I stay in control, the staff accepts me as their leader. I'm afraid that if I let go of the control, they might not accept me, or even like me, and nothing would get done."

It is only when we risk vulnerability and even rejection, that we not only begin to do the real work of the Lord but that we ourselves are changed so that we too are developing into the persons God wants us to become.

Ways We Control

We control the ministry and people in many obvious and subtle ways.

We make all the decisions. The more decisions that must come through us the more we control the ministry and the more we suppress our people's creativity. The ministry must move at our pace and adjust to our availability to see people; listen to their ideas; read their proposals; and consider the alternatives, the consequences, and the costs. Some dreams may never be born, not because they were bad ideas but because they took too long to get to us or we took too long deliberating over them. One church missed out on an opportunity to get two hundred much-needed student desks for free from a private school that was going out of business. They had to notify the school immediately if they wanted the desks but the church had a policy that no donations could be accepted without the pastor's personal approval. He was out of town for three days.

We keep information to ourselves. Nadia doesn't have staff meetings. Her people report individually to her and she doesn't share those reports with other staff members. Fairly often, staff members find out that they could have saved time and energy had they known that one of the other people had already researched something, tried something, or knew someone. But Nadia feels that to have her people network with each other would jeopardize her control.

We develop contingency plans. Scott gives the appearance of letting his people own their ministries; however, his is a very subtle form of control. Scott always has a contingency plan to impose on the people if something starts to go wrong, as it usually does! So they end up doing things Scott's way after all.

It would be better if Scott asked questions of the people up front, such as "what will you do if . . . ," and let them plan for their own contingencies. In that way the people would be developing planning skills.

We share our own dreams too quickly. Rachael schedules planning meetings with her people and initiates discussions about new ministries, encouraging them to share ideas and possibilities. However, not all of the people who come to the planning meetings have thought in advance about the new ministry opportunities. Thus they are not prepared to immediately come up with terrific ideas. Rachael, on the other hand, has usually spent a great deal of time thinking and praying about the possibility of a new ministry, so she is full of good ideas.

If Rachael shares her ideas too quickly, the group input will be seriously curtailed and they may be tempted to simply adopt her vision, when they might have come up with a better idea had they all contributed.

We procrastinate. Drew is a master procrastinator. He jokingly says he believes in the Crock-Pot theory of leadership: "Just put everything on the back burner and ignore it. It will either take care of itself, or it will boil over. If it boils over it is important and I deal with it."

We can control very effectively by simply procrastinating about having meetings, approving plans, signing forms, meeting people, listening to dreams, affirming people, and so on.

However, procrastination is one of the control techniques that frustrates people the most. Some would rather hear a "no" than be held in limbo forever.

We eliminate the unpredictable. Sandra hates surprises. She has operating procedures to cover every contingency. The other day a staff member had a car accident in the parking lot, knocking over a potted tree. Within three hours there was a neatly typed procedure in the book, outlining the steps staff should follow if this should ever happen again. The nursery telephone number was included as well as the anticipated cost of replacing each tree in the parking lot.

Sandra doesn't often trust people to know what to do or to depend on their common sense or creativity. By eliminating the unpredictable, Sandra controls people, stifling their ministries in many ways.

While there's nothing wrong with being prepared, if we try to totally eliminate the mystery and the unpredictable from life, we may have a greater problem. We will spend too much time planning for the negative and worrying about the what-if's instead of the more positive could-be's.

We withhold affirmation or encouragement. Whenever people come to Richard excited about a new idea, he listens, sort of frowns, and shakes his head thoughtfully. More often than not he'll say, "I don't know. Let me think about it." Countless dream embryos die in Richard's office simply because his initial response is so negative that people lose confidence and abandon their dreams.

One of the most powerful tools leaders have is the ability to affirm and encourage. To withhold affirmation or encouragement is a tremendous act of control. Even if we think the idea is terrible, we can affirm the person's creativity and commitment and encourage him or her to work through some of the dream's possible problems. Instead of controlling we can encourage and affirm our people and release them to fulfill their dreams.

When We Don't Control

The first step in relinquishing control is acknowledging that our struggle is a spiritual battle and our greatest challenge is that ". . . our struggle is not against flesh and blood, but against the rulers, against the authorities, against the powers of this dark world and against the spiritual forces of evil in the heavenly realms" (Eph. 6:12). God is sovereign. He is in charge of the battle, the war, and the guaranteed ultimate victory! Our sin occurs when we dare to usurp that authority and to presume that the Holy Spirit who gives us ideas and dreams is different from or somehow better than the Holy Spirit who gives ideas and dreams to our people. When we insist on control, we are not only saying that we don't trust our people, we are saying that we don't trust God.

God understands that we operate best when we are dependent on him, rather than taking control ourselves. Look at the Old Testament stories of how he provided for people in a way that ensured daily dependence. Manna for the Israelites. Ravens for Elijah. The cruse of oil and handful of meal for the widow, her son, and the prophet.

We often have a tendency to tell God that we can handle some things so he needn't bother. Usually this is when we are afraid God might not do something the way we want it! We try to push programs through the decisioning process or we try to bring about changes on our own rather than praying that God will work with divine timing and intervention. But whenever we are brought to a position where we are clearly beyond our own powers to resolve a problem, we turn to God and find him ready, willing, and able to take effective charge. Why do we wait so long?

Look what happens when people try to do things their way, to jump in and give God a helping hand. Moses struck the rock, not trusting God to respond to his spoken word to the rock, and Moses never saw the promised land. Abraham took Hagar to have a son when he was unsure that God would provide a child through Sarah. This resulted in not only the alienation of Hagar and her son from Abraham's family, but also an enmity between the descendants of Ishmael and Isaac, which persists to this day.

What happens when we do give up control? God's power gives glorious results! Remember Gideon, who recruited thirty-two thousand men to fight against the Midianites, a formidable enemy that greatly outnumbered them. God said, "Too many," and twenty-two thousand were sent home because they were fearful, and nine thousand seven hundred more were sent home because they were not watchful as they drank water. Gideon was left with three hundred men—and God. Of course, they won the battle (without swords). What a victory!

Whenever we let God step in, the results are usually miraculous and remind us that we serve a loving, all-powerful God.

When we let go, we begin to experience real intimacy with our people and with God. We can establish intimacy with our people because we are no longer setting ourselves up as the expert, the master, or the manager. We are just one of the members of the team. We are vulnerable. We can be accepted *or* rejected. We are taking risks. People are seeing us without the protective armor of our control.

We experience increased intimacy with God because we are more dependent on him and therefore more in touch with what he would have us do. When we let go of control, other people are freed up to grow, to risk, to expand their dreams into real live ministries to reach others for Christ.

We All Struggle

Everyone struggles to some extent with control issues. For some it is an ongoing war, for others just an occasional battle. Curbing our natural desire to control can be an act of daily obedience to God's will in our lives. When we let go, we discover the adventure that leadership was meant to be.

Domination

Who Has the Power?

Power is difficult to keep in balance. Too little power and we are ineffective; too much and we are despotic. Neither of these extremes is good. What is the balance of power that leaders need to be effective? It's not always easy to determine. If we define power as *the ability to exercise our will,* it can be good when we are choosing for ourselves and bad when we are attempting to impose our will and choose for others.

The Holy Spirit enables us to give away power and empower others in ministry, which releases the power of the Holy Spirit in more people. This is the cycle. Who has the power, his power? We do.

Positive Aspects of Power

"No problem. I can take care of that for you. It will be ready in the morning." Lashanda smiled at one of her leaders, who had come to her with what seemed like a major obstacle. She would be able to resolve the problem by providing her assistance, support, and knowledge. The ministry continued, unblocked by minor problems. That's a positive use of power. What are others?

Helping People in Need

When someone comes to us in need, we don't necessarily try to satisfy all of his or her needs or to remove all of the challenges in his or her life. Helping people often means "coming alongside" and sharing the journey for a while.

Dave was a runner who had trained for a fifteen-kilometer race in the Los Angeles area. He had a strategy for the race. He was going to run the first half at a nice, steady pace, and then pour on the steam for the last half. The day of the race dawned and it was perfect. He felt great. The race started and Dave put his plan into action. He ran the first half at a steady pace and was preparing to speed up to finish the last half when the road turned and went straight uphill!

Dave groaned aloud and muttered to himself that he couldn't make it up the hill. He started to drop out of the race altogether when a friend came up from behind and said, "Come on Dave, I'll pace it with you."

The friend could have said "I'll run behind you and kick your heels!" and Dave would have been angry. The guy could have said "I'll stand on the side of the road and cheer you on" and Dave would have said "no thanks." But what the friend said was perfect. And Dave found new strength as his friend matched his steps to Dave's. Step by step they climbed the hill together and finished the race.

The Holy Spirit is our *parakletos*, which means "one who comes alongside to help" (see John 14:16). When you come

alongside, you don't go where you want people to be—
you go where they are and walk their journey with them.
There is great strength and power in pacing life together.

Providing Necessary Information

Information is power! If you know how to do something, you can usually do it. If you know how the system
works, you can work the system. If you know the right
people, you can frequently facilitate the operation of the
ministry.

Leaders can inappropriately use information power by
withholding information so that everyone must come to
them for instruction or by giving more information than
is needed or wanted, which can be confusing. (For example, you ask the leader what time it is and he or she tells
you how to make a clock!) Leaders who instantly give pat
answers to personal problems, quick solutions to any problem, and instant reactions to ideas and who must be first
to share their own dreams are misusing their power.

There are many times, however, when a leader's knowledge can be of tremendous assistance to the people in ministry. Teaching and preaching are good examples of productive uses of knowledge. Counseling techniques, policies
and procedures, and the Scriptures are all useful tools for
the leader who wants to assist people in building their
dreams.

Removing Obstacles to Dreams

Lars was an associate pastor at a church that had a
strict policy of no food in the sanctuary. Someone came
to him with a dream of a unique outreach, a onetime
event that included serving food in the sanctuary to those
who came to the event. There was no other place at the

church large enough to hold the number of people anticipated to attend.

Lars saw the possibilities of the dream and with some negotiation and compromises about the types of food served, was able to convince the church board to make an exception to the policy for the one event.

We are not called to be snowplows, to go out in front of our people and indiscriminately remove all obstacles from their paths. However, we are called to be of assistance and to support those under our leadership.

Creating a Safe Environment for Risk Taking

"Before we start the discussion tonight, let's agree on the ground rules," Carmen said. "Everyone has a right to his/her own opinion. No ideas are stupid. Take ownership for your ideas and comments. No put-downs . . ."

Carmen was creating a safe environment for sharing ideas and dreams. Many people are, by nature and practice, judgmental, critical, and belittling. They can quickly kill people's dreams and their willingness to risk. A good leader learns early to set ground rules for brainstorming sessions, for group discussions, and for trying out new ideas. By giving people permission to make mistakes, to suggest something that may not work, and to share what they're really thinking, leaders enable people to grow and develop new skills.

Intervening in Blocked Relationships

Carlos shares, "For months I had watched two of my deacons lock horns and butt heads. Regardless of the issue, they always took opposite sides, when sometimes they really weren't that far apart. Finally, I knew I had to do something because the friction was beginning to adversely affect our total ministry. I prayed long and hard about how to handle the situation. Then I asked the two deacons to come to my office for a meeting. I shared with them what I had observed in their behavior and its impact on the church. I invited them to share with each other what was troubling them, what they saw as a problem in their relationship, what they wanted from each other, and what they were willing to contribute to the relationship. At first it was awkward and I was afraid we were getting nowhere. Then one man opened up and confessed he had been jealous and angry over the other's appointment to the finance committee. That broke the logjam and soon a number of misunderstandings were shared. After two hours they left my office ready to work together."

Sometimes a leader has to do the hard task of confronting people who are blocking the ministry with nonproductive attitudes and behaviors. We must be willing to prepare carefully (and prayerfully) for this and speak the truth in love (see Eph. 4:15). We need to phrase our confrontations in nonthreatening and productive ways that allow people to confess and express their feelings in order to resolve problems in relationships.

Renaming People

"I think one of the most powerful things a leader can do is to help people rename themselves!" Teresa says, then goes on to explain, "A lot of people think of themselves in negative terms. 'I'm a klutz' they say. Or 'I'm shy,' 'I'm forgetful,' or 'I'm incapable.' A good leader can rename people and help them have successful experiences that will change their self-given labels to names like 'graceful,' 'bold,' 'capable,' and a 'person of a good memory'!"

We agree. That's what God does for us. He gives us a new name as we are created new creatures in him.

Remember in the Bible how God changed people's names?

From	To
Abram (high)	Abraham (multitude)—Genesis 17:5
Sarai (contentious)	Sarah (princess)—Genesis 17:5
Jacob (supplanter)	Israel (prince with God)—Genesis 32:28
Simon (a hearkening)	Peter (a stone)—Matthew 16:18
Saul (asked for)	Paul (little)—Acts 13:9

When we help people redefine their self-concepts to include new skills, new abilities, and a new willingness to take risks, we are using power in a very positive way.

Blessing People

The dictionary says that blessing people is to praise them, to call them holy, or to call God's favor upon them. As leaders we have a great deal of power with which to bless people. We can affirm and encourage them with our words, our attitudes, our belief in them, and our support. We can reward with praise, challenge to holiness by our example and exhortation, and provide a system of accountability for them to help them in their walk. And perhaps more important, we can hold up our people to God in prayer on a daily basis, asking that he confer his favor on them and their dream.

Empowering Others

"One of the most powerful people I know is always giving power to others," Adam marvels.

It's true that one of the ways to exercise power in a positive way is to give the power away. The more we draw others into our circles and the more people we release and empower to visualize their dreams, the more powerful we become personally, in the right way.

It seems that almost everything we receive from God is to be given away. We receive salvation and are sent to share our faith (Matt. 28:19, 20). We receive spiritual gifts to edify others (Eph. 4:11–13). We receive comfort to comfort others (2 Cor. 1:3–5). And we are given power to empower others to ministry (Eph. 3:16–20).

Negative Connotations of Power

"I shy away from seeking power," says Jon. "I've always equated power with negative images, like Hitler."

Jon is not alone. One of the reasons we are not more powerful in our ministries is that we think all power is bad and that power corrupts. How many of the following terms come to mind when you think of power?

pushy	isolated	authoritarian
selfish	self-centered	tough
ramrodding	controlling	loud
roughshod	steamroller	despotic
uncaring	bossy	domineering
arbitrary	tyrannous	demanding

Certainly these terms are descriptive of people who exercise the wrong kinds of power. When we set out to get things done *our* way, regardless of the cost or anyone standing in our way, we are in danger of misusing power.

Ways We Make People Powerless

Many leaders wish their people were competent and creative but these leaders actually behave in ways designed to keep the people powerless.

We keep the power. No matter what they may say, some people do not believe that the people should be set free to minister. These leaders cherish the belief that only one person should have the power, make the decisions, resolve the problems, and do the work of the ministry. Consequently, they attempt to keep the power for themselves, limiting the ministry.

We protect the people. Some leaders are born rescuers. They take care of people in a smothering way that stifles creativity. They make decisions for people, they talk for them, they tell them what to do and when to do it, and they don't let people take any risks.

We act as perpetual mentors. Mentoring is wonderful and a very critical step in empowering others. But there comes a time when we must let go and allow the protégé to take a few risks on his or her own. Insisting on being a perpetual mentor makes the protégé powerless.

We resist changes. Leaders who are resistant to new ideas or changes suggested by others are ensuring that the people stay in their little ruts forever. Insisting that things always go their way and remain as they are, some leaders guard their power jealously, making their people feel helpless to improve the ministry.

We are perfectionistic. A few leaders have discovered that they can retain all the power if they simply insist that before any new dreams are attempted, there must be perfect plans in place and near guarantees of success. Soon the people stop dreaming of new ways to minister because their leader is a "dreambuster." The people are powerless.

There are a few payoffs for the leader who insists on keeping people powerless. That leader gets things done his or her way. The leader eliminates lengthy discussions and planning sessions. The leader always knows what's happening in the ministry. The leader is definitely in charge.

However, the price that leader pays is high indeed. The people stop envisioning their dreams, and Proverbs 29:18 says that "Where there is no vision, the people perish" (KJV). People no longer voice creative ideas and instead of a body of people carrying the work of the ministry, there is only one leader to do everything. The ministry must stay small if everything is to be controlled by one person. Outreach will suffer. People who might have otherwise been reached won't be. The ministry will grow stale and parts will die off due to a lack of circulation of new ideas and fresh interests. There will be no growing and changing to meet the needs of a changing people. The people will feel alienated from the leader and will take no ownership of the ministry. The leader will lack support and affirmation. The people will become dependent on the leader for everything.

Empowering People

There are several ways you can help empower your people to reach their full potential as ministers for God.

Information Power

Knowledge is powerful. When people come to you with their dreams, encourage them to go find out everything they can about what it would take to make those dreams come true. Are zoning regulations a problem? How can they be changed? Are any permits or licenses required? How does the system work? Who else has done something similar? What problems did they encounter? How were those problems solved? Are there any books or articles on the subject? Who would be good resource people to contact?

Turn people loose to discover the answers to their questions from sources other than you. Don't confine their dreams to the limits of your knowledge.

Learn to help people ask good questions and then research the answers as they explore their dreams. The more they know, the easier it will be to make the right decisions in birthing their dreams.

Charisma Power

Encourage people to develop the power to inspire devotion and enthusiasm in others. A wise leader doesn't try to keep all of the devotion, loyalty, and enthusiasm coming his or her way. Instead, a wise leader knows that when people develop the ability to gather loyal, committed teams around them, the ministry will grow and become strong.

Encourage people to develop close relationships with their team members; to experience the intimacy of sharing dreams, goals, failures, and feelings. As people dream together and work together on ministry, commitment to one another and to the ministry will increase.

Position Power

We can empower people by giving them a title and allowing them to assume the authority to make decisions. Also we need to stand behind people when decisions they've made prove not to be the best ones. Too often people are called "coordinators," when all they are allowed to coordinate is the carrying out of the decisions of the leader.

Giving people permission to try new things, risk a few failures, and experiment with different styles is truly an empowering function of leadership.

Relational Power

Few of us can survive in this world without a group of close friends. In ministry we also need the small group. As we relate to one another in an open, vulnerable, and caring way, we invest in one another's lives. The body is strengthened and each individual becomes more powerful because of the support of the group.

Encourage people to become a member of a caring small group. Intimate relationships affirm our strengths, point out our weaknesses, encourage our growth efforts, and prod us out of ruts. Kind honesty is something we all need if we are to stand powerfully in a world of broken trust and pain.

Spiritual Power

The most important source of power for people is, of course, the Lord. And while we can't take responsibility for giving that power to them, we can, if we aren't careful, block their receiving or using that power. What does the Bible say about power?

Isaiah 40:29	God gives power to the faint.
John 1:12	God gives power to become children of the Almighty.
Acts 1:8	God gives us power through the Holy Spirit.
Romans 13:1	God gives all power that is given.

Ephesians 3:20	God can do . . . according to the power that works in us.
2 Samuel 22:33	God is our strength and power.
1 Peter 2:24	God has healing power.
Matthew 10:1	God gives power over unclean spirits.
Luke 10:19	God gives power over the enemy.
Luke 24:49	God sends the Holy Spirit to empower us.
Romans 15:13	God gives hope through power of the Holy Spirit.
1 Corinthians 7:37	God gives power over our will.
Ephesians 3:7	God gives ministries through his divine power.
Galatians 6:7–9	God gives power to make choices.

Nowhere in these verses does it say that the power is strictly limited to leaders. The promises are there for the claiming. A wise leader will want to empower the people to expand the ministry through God's power.

Dignity

How Do We Keep Score?

The single adult program at the church was very small, usually there were only six to eight people in the Sunday class. There were two members who had started the class because of their own experiences following painful divorces. The other attendees were generally people who were struggling through problems related to being single. They would attend the class for two or three months, then, feeling stronger, they would integrate back into other adult programs; they were hurting people, quietly healed by love and released to reach out to others.

Most of the "graduates" of the single adult class had strong, positive self-images, had dealt with forgiveness issues, and were ready to become active in the work of the church. While attending the single adult class, they had been cared for, affirmed, heard, and prayed for and had enjoyed the fellowship. The class was known for the loving support of its members. They often got together on

Saturdays and helped each other with major chores while easing the pain of loneliness. There were always one or two new people who had heard of the class and would start attending at about the time one of the members moved on.

What an unpleasant surprise it was when the pastor, referring to the frequent member turnover, was overheard saying, "our singles program is not really successful." Well, that depends on how you keep score!

Why We Keep Score

From a very early age we were given messages that we must behave in certain ways in order to be accepted and loved. We were told to be smart, good, strong, cute, quiet, and a thousand other things. Sometimes the messages were confusing and conflicting and we didn't always do a good job of sorting through them. The overt message defined acceptable behavior. The inferred message was that we had to be perfect or we would not be loved.

Soon we learned to check how we were doing based on people's responses to us and how others treated us. The more positive feedback we received, the more we believed ourselves loved. We believed that if we achieved more, we would receive more recognition (and love). A lifetime habit of keeping score was born.

A second reason we keep score is because almost everyone else does it! Some people not only keep their scores (and publish them regularly) but are also very good at keeping ours too and letting us know how we are doing in their estimation. In response, some leaders reluctantly start keeping score in self-defense, then get hooked forever.

Another reason we keep score is that we secretly feel that we are less than competent in ministry and are afraid someone will find us out. So we try to build up as many tangible proofs as possible that we are successful, to fight off possible rejection and criticism.

We also keep score because we have failed to take the time to set specific goals and objectives for our ministries and instead use inappropriate ways to measure our success. Success can be defined as the degree to which we reach our stated goals. If these goals are clear, measurable, reachable, and dated, a leader will be able to know how well he or she is doing at any given point without playing scorekeeping games.

Games We Play

Instead of admitting that we are imperfect human beings called by God to be leaders, we often try to play games and hide behind various masks.

Everything's fine! Dennis wears a perpetual smile. His response to "How are you?" is an enthusiastic, "Fantabulous!" Neither the response nor the smile is real. Actually Dennis feels overwhelmed and anxious much of the time. Only when he is able to admit these feelings will he be able to relate on a genuine level and receive the real love he wants.

Everything's under control! Yvonne is an extremely competent leader. She appears unflappable. People don't mind running to her with last-minute crises because they know she can handle anything. Inside, Yvonne is scared that one day something will go wrong and she will fail as a leader. She doesn't have much help on projects because she wants everything done right—her way.

I don't need approval! Brett tries to pretend that he doesn't need approval from others as long as he is doing what he thinks is right. That's partly true. But we do need the approval of at least our small group or our best friends in order to check ourselves and to keep from going off on nonproductive tangents. We all need some degree of approval from people we love, respect, and trust.

How We Keep Score

Leaders tend to keep score in many ways. It's true that certain accomplishments may temporarily make us feel as if we are winners in the race for success. However, if we allow ourselves to judge ministry effectiveness on wrong criteria, we may miss out on the good thing that God has in store for us. What are some of the wrong criteria?

Note: There is nothing wrong with enjoying the following achievements, they are definitely ego boosting. It must be remembered, however, that they are not the most significant factors in the ministry.

Numbers

"We had three hundred junior highers at our retreat. That's double what we had last year!" Lana exclaims excitedly, feeling very successful.

Numbers are a good measure of how successful your publicity is, how attractive or intriguing your program is, how charismatic your speaker is, and what type of reputation your church or group has. It is usually more fun to have one hundred people at an event than five. And numbers *may* indicate how well your program is meeting the needs of those who attend.

The problem with depending on numbers as a criterion is that some ministries are more effective in small groups, where even one person affected is worthwhile. Leaders who fall in love with numerical success may terminate a highly effective small program, not realizing that large numbers are not the only indicators of success.

Recognition

"I'll know I'm successful when I go to a national pastor's conference and even the new people will know who I am or at least will have heard my name," Neil acknowledges.

What a thrill to walk into a new situation and have people affirm us! Leaders who measure their worth by recognition will often focus their efforts on high publicity events. Their names are on the church sign and their pictures are in the weekly bulletins and church ads in the newspaper. They must be up front at every service, actively leading meetings and events. Keeping score by recognition means the leader won't be developing people by letting them assume leadership roles.

Church "Perks"

A large church was recruiting for a new associate pastor. At last they found the person they were searching for. He was flown to the church and treated royally for a weekend. He was promised a large salary, a large office, and the loan of a new car every year from a local car dealer who was a member of the church. His parking place would be right out front.

When the prospective pastor met the person whose office he would be given, he protested that the office changes weren't necessary. "Oh, yes they are," the man replied.

"You must have this office. We want people to know how important you are!"

There's no question that perks are terrific to get or that we enjoy them. They are often an indicator of how appreciative people are of us. But leaders who choose ministries based on what they offer as perquisites may be missing God's call in their lives. Don't forget that being given a nice car and being sent on an all-expenses-paid vacation by the church are not necessarily indicators that we are successfully developing people or releasing them to minister to others.

Type of Congregation

Will's inner-city church is attended by two hundred people who are a mix of street people, young unwed mothers on welfare, and laborers. There is a tremendous spirit of worship and joy in the services and people leave feeling loved and challenged to make life changes.

Josh's church is in the suburbs and is attended by about two hundred people, mostly professionals. The offerings are substantial and there are a lot of programs listed in the bulletin. The atmosphere is formal and somewhat cold. Yet many people would say that Josh's ministry is more successful than Will's simply because of the type of people in the congregation. This is not true. Ministry is about reaching people, all people, not just those who are wealthy, educated, professional, or socially elite.

Sophistication of the Outreach

Radio programs, television shows, lavish stage productions, musical concerts, famous guest speakers, and terrific Christmas programs are all great ways to let the world know that the church exists and to draw in the unchurched.

However, when each year's events have to be bigger and better and cost more than those of previous years, the leaders may be headed in the wrong direction. The real success of any outreach is in how many people are reached; how many lives are changed.

The Church Building

"I'm not sure where to draw the line between functional and aesthetic when it comes to the new church building!" Dayana admits. "On one hand it would be terrific to worship in a beautiful sanctuary, but we could use the extra money to build a gym. The outreach potential of having a gym is unlimited!"

Sometimes we need to take a look at what we are planning and what we are using to keep score when it comes to building programs and facilities. Making it beautiful is good. Making it effective for ministry is better.

Affirmation

Some pastors thrive on affirmation and don't feel they are successful unless they are constantly affirmed by their people. They hope for compliments at the door at the end of the service, for cards and letters during the week, for plaques at the church anniversary dinner, and for special love offerings at least twice a year. They appreciate being asked to speak at other churches and conferences and they feel unsuccessful if these things don't happen.

Affirmation is wonderful. We all need it. But our self-esteem cannot be based on the approval of others. We have already received the highest affirmation—we are ". . . accepted in the beloved" (Eph. 1:6 KJV). Besides, people are fickle. They may appreciate you today because they agree with your approach but withhold affirmation from you tomorrow if you have had to take a tough stand or teach a lesson that struck too close to home!

Status

"I'm called a 'coordinator of children's programs,' and I really hate that title. I'll know I've arrived when I'm called the 'children's pastor.' *Pastor* sounds better than *coordinator*," Maurice confesses.

Some people do keep score by relative status in the organization. Titles, membership on select committees, and possession of church keys are some of the indicators we use to check whether or not we have status.

Attaining status is fine unless it becomes the driving force in a leader's decision making and choice of activity.

Achievement

Cho can list the twenty-three specifically different accomplishments she has achieved in her ministry in the last five months. Cho will always get a lot accomplished because that is how she keeps score. She can match her record favorably against anyone's! She does more, more often, than most other leaders in positions similar to hers.

Accomplishment is a goal most of us strive toward. But sometimes, as in Cho's case, the need to accomplish bigger and better things can cloud our judgment and cause us to make ministry mistakes.

Appearance

Franz is a six-foot-one, 175-pound leader who works out at the gym at least three nights a week and eats a perfectly healthful diet. He dresses impeccably and makes a terrific first impression. Franz's primary assessment of any potential new leader is physical: How would this person look in front of a group? He has discouraged involvement by overweight women and balding men because they don't fit the mental picture he has of successful leaders.

Caring for the body as a temple of the Holy Spirit is commendable. Excluding people from ministry because they don't look perfect, isn't.

Relationships

Lucy collects relationships to feel successful. She always manages to sit with the guest speaker, chat with the guest musical artist, or become best friends with the pastor's wife. She likes to feel important by knowing "important" people. Lucy won't join a small care group unless it has "special" people in it.

There is a difference between being a genuinely friendly person who loves to get to know others and being a people collector like Lucy.

A Better Approach

If we are to break out of lifelong habits and quit keeping score, we need a better approach to evaluating how we are doing in the ministry.

Remember whose approval is important. Paul reminds us in Galatians 1:10 that our priorities come from God and it is his approval we must seek. If we are doing what God wants us to do, then even if nearly everyone else thinks we're wrong, we can feel okay, knowing that we are pleasing him.

Acknowledge our imperfections. We often find that when we let down our guard and allow people to see us as we really are, faults and all, they will rally around with affirmation and affection. As long as we pretend to be perfect and strong, we are keeping ourselves from growing and others from ministering to us.

Focus on others. Keeping score usually means we are focusing on ourselves. We are checking how much attention, affirmation, affection, and approval we are getting and how many people are noticing. A successful leader takes what good things come to him or her but actually focuses on what God is doing in, through, and for others. Do we notice that:

> Ron can stand up in front of a group now when he was petrified to do so three months ago?
>
> Rhonda is able to trust men again after her rejection experience last year?
>
> Brad, who used to be rude and obnoxious, treats people courteously now?
>
> Ellen has begun an outreach program for the children in her neighborhood?
>
> Doug gives two full evenings a week to ministry, when last year he couldn't be coaxed away from his television set during the week?

If our goal is developing people, our success is best measured by what God has done in their lives and what new ministries have begun through others.

When evaluating how successful we are in ministry we also have to keep in mind that people develop and grow at their own pace, not necessarily at the pace we wish them to!

Maintain a positive self-image. Recognizing and accepting who we are and where we are in our journeys are the first two steps in developing a positive self-image. It is only when we accept where we are that we can begin to make life changes toward where we want to be. Setting goals for personal development is the next step and working on those goals moves us farther along in our quest for self-esteem.

On the other hand, there is also a need to acknowledge that each person is a valuable human being. Each of us is, as Dr. Robert Schuller says, "a unique, unrepeatable miracle of God"! We are valued by God, loved by God, and empowered through the Holy Spirit to do God's work.

Paul says, "we are God's workmanship, created in Christ Jesus to do good works, which God prepared in advance for us to do" (Eph. 2:10). Don't keep score, walk in his love.

Distress

How Do We Keep Cool?

Howard and Ramón were associate pastors at a large church. Their workload was fairly equal, but while Ramón seemed to be coping well and appeared relaxed, Howard was stressed out and appeared to be inundated with work. One day Howard walked into Ramón's office and exploded, "If one more thing goes wrong, I'm going to go stark, raving mad! How do you stay so cool?"

"It's a long story, Howard. It's called effective stress management."

What Is Stress?

Ministers who are constantly involved in the high-pressure politics and activities of the church, the denomination, and the community are often warned by friends that if they don't slow down and learn to relax, the stress will kill them. Others admit to being under stress when faced with too many needs and too few resources. These pastors often suffer from tension headaches and other stress-related physical problems.

Many people have the idea that stress is an external force over which people have little control. However, a look at the research findings on stress reveal the surprising truth that stress is actually the body's internal response to external changes.

Change is a fact of life. Our world is in a constant state of change. Political liaisons are formed and broken in quick succession. Revolutions give birth to new revolutions. Nothing seems stable.

Our society is perhaps the most changeable in the world. New technology and research seem to affect our lives in new ways on a daily basis. Each year thousands of laws are passed, regulations adopted, and court decisions made that affect our lives. Each year we have to relearn how to compute our income taxes. Fashions, fads, music, and standards are constantly changing.

Our immediate social world changes. Close friends move away. A coworker takes a new job. A neighbor dies. Friends divorce.

Our relationships change. We miscommunicate, argue, and grow apart. We experience a rare moment of shared intimacy. A casual friend becomes a close buddy. We experience rejection and betrayal or acceptance and love, and sometimes all in the same relationship.

Some changes are ministry related. We change churches or responsibilities. New staff members are added, others leave. The emphasis of the ministry shifts. The demands on our time become more excessive and insistent. Communications break down. Priorities collide. Unrealistic expectations cause tension to build between staff members as they strive to complete their assignments while sharing limited resources.

Some changes are self-imposed. We tell ourselves we should be better, we should do or know more. We determine to get a better position. We decide we must change how we act, look, or think. In order to meet these personal challenges, we initiate changes in our everyday lives. We work to acquire new knowledge, skills, or abilities. We go on a diet, upgrade our lifestyle, or assume new financial obligations. We experiment with different approaches to the various circumstances that exist within our daily lives. We move, change jobs, or join a new small group. We make a new friend. We forgive, let go, and move on.

Each change triggers a physiological response, however slight, in our body systems. Therefore we are constantly processing our responses to the thousands of stressors we experience each day. Much of the time we are unaware of either the stressor or our response to it because the body functions so automatically. However, if our exposure to the stressor becomes constant or increases in intensity, our stress response, in an effort to compensate, increases to an uncomfortable level.

Consider, for example, entering a dimly lit room and turning on a lamp. You may not be acutely aware of the adjustment your pupils make to the change in the amount of light in the room. However, if you were in a very dark room and someone were to repeatedly turn on a very bright spotlight, your body's response would be more intense. You might blink, see red spots, or have a sharp headache as your eyes adjusted to the dramatic change. Controlling the body's response to the stressor would be as simple as closing your eyes or leaving the light either on or off. Controlling the stress response to the many changes listed above is not always that easy because often we cannot control the timing or stop the changes that are occurring and neither can we remove ourselves from the stressors. So we must learn to manage the stress response by developing effective coping skills and strengths.

The body responds automatically to changes. We get goosebumps if the room temperature is too cold and we perspire when it is too hot. The body's response to a small change is usually unnoticeable. The real problems arise when a number of small changes build up and the effect is cumulative.

Lea was stressed out the other day. She started the morning with a disagreement with her daughter over her school outfit, ran out of gas on the way to work, and found a note on her desk saying that her secretary was out on jury duty. She was under pressure to have her final budget request computed, typed, and turned in by the noon deadline. After a third coworker interrupted her with a petty "emergency," she lost control. "Leave me alone!" she shrieked, causing the coworker to burst into tears.

Lea could have handled any one of those little stressors without a problem. It was the accumulated stress of responding to several changes that pushed her past her limit.

A variation of this effect is when exposure to one small stressor continues over a long period of time and the stress response is prolonged. This is the "last straw" syndrome. A staff member is known for losing his copy of anything and everything. His boss gets annoyed but is usually somewhat tolerant. If, however, the staff member loses the only copy of an important contract, his boss may respond by firing him. The repeated annoyances may have built up a low tolerance in the boss and when a loss of something extremely important occurs, the boss overreacts.

The Stress Response

The body's physical and chemical responses to stress date back to primitive days when a primary stressor was physical danger. Today's "dangers," although usually more psychological than physical, are just as taxing.

Whatever the source, the body responds in three stages of a process that Dr. Hans Selye calls the "general adaption syndrome" (GAS).[1]

In the first stage, "alarm," the hypothalamus (a small portion of the brain) sends a message to the pituitary gland that the body is under attack. The pituitary gland releases a hormone, ACTH, into the bloodstream. When the ACTH gets to the adrenal glands, they react by increasing the levels of adrenaline and corticoids in the bloodstream. This brings the body to an aroused state within eight seconds of the initial alarm. Meanwhile the heart, lungs, and muscles have been alerted that the person may have to fight or run (called the "fight or flight" response). The blood pressure rises slightly as the blood is directed away from the extremities to the larger muscles in the arms and legs. The liver speeds up the conversion of glycogen to glucose. The breathing becomes more rapid. The heart pumps harder and the skeletal muscles brace to be ready to fight or run. The digestive system shuts down, often producing indigestion (and ulcers if the stress response is prolonged). Thinking in the abstract becomes more difficult. Hearing is more acute and vision more sensitive.

All of these things occur very quickly if the stressor is major. If you learn that someone you care deeply about has just been in a serious accident, within seconds you may experience a rush of adrenaline with subsequent shortness of breath, upset stomach, cold hands and feet, and headache. The noise of the secretary's typewriter seems suddenly too loud and intrusive. This is the stress response in action.

The second stage is called "resistance." During this phase the body makes adjustments to be able to cope with the symptoms of the alarm stage. The body can temporarily cope with the loss of circulation to the extremities, the stalled digestive system, and the other physiological changes that occur during the alarm stage. The energy drain is phenomenal but not acutely felt at first. If the resistance phase lasts too long, the individual's reserves get used up and he or she begins to experience symptoms of stress overload. When we are in a stress overload situation, we find that even the most insignificant demand can suddenly become the proverbial last straw.

Somewhere along the way we have used up our flexibility, our coping strength, and have begun to run on reserve energy. Watch for these signs that you are using up your reserve.

- Little interruptions to your schedule or small demands become impossible obstacles. Their existence seems like a deliberate, personal attack. You know that the plumber didn't deliberately decide not to show up after you took the entire day off from work just to wait for him. He probably had an emergency. But you *feel* that somehow you were singled out to be inconvenienced.
- Paradoxically, while little things seem to immobilize you, major problems seem almost insignificant and are often easily resolved.
- You experience some of the following warning signs of near exhaustion: excessive irritability, fatigue, change in sleeping habits, intestinal disturbances, weight change, respiration problems, irregularities of the heartbeat, depression, general dissatisfaction, inability to make decisions, apathy, and a loss of creativity.

Perhaps one of the easiest ways to recognize that we are starting to operate in the danger zone is a nagging conviction that if too many more things go wrong, we won't be able to cope. Until we cross over into our reserve, the question of whether or not we can cope doesn't enter our minds. We feel capable and strong.

Unfortunately we tend to live up to the very limits of our resources. Our schedules are so full that we can't fit in unexpected delays or demands. Often we accept more stressors than we can reasonably handle, which forces us to operate on our reserve energies on a regular basis. As a result we are left without the energy resources to cope effectively with unexpected stressors.

After the resistance stage, the body enters the third and final stage, "exhaustion," which can lead to forced rest, illness, and even, if not checked, death.

When GAS is triggered, the body's natural state of balance is upset as energy is diverted from other areas to support the stress response. If the stress is short-lived, the body's systems quickly rebalance and return to homeostasis. If the stress is prolonged, sufficient energy to maintain a healthy body is no longer available and illness may occur. The physical symptoms will vary, depending on an individual's inherited predisposition for disease. The more common illnesses or symptoms are insomnia, headaches, colds, flu, allergies, impotence, ulcers, colitis, asthma, dermatitis, hypertension, premature aging, bronchitis, emphysema, diabetes, heart disease, tuberculosis, and even cancer, according to recent research.

Other Changes

When the body is experiencing stress, and all of the concomitant physiological changes, there are resultant changes in other life areas also.

Emotional Changes

People under stress often experience feelings of insecurity and fearfulness. Tempers flare and moods swing from exhilaration to depression with alarming speed. Minor problems trigger major responses and reactions. There is an increased need for love and affection but often there is a paradoxical intolerance for touching as they reject even hugs as being "too confining." Because all of their coping strength is being self-directed, stressed people aren't very patient with others. Some take their irritability out on those around them while others just hide out and begin to sleep for as much of the day as they can.

Psychological Changes

People experiencing stress overload often notice that their self-concepts change. A normally confident person may experience serious self-doubt. A capable person may feel incompetent; a strong person, weak; and an independent person, dependent. Teresa is normally a strong, independent lady who has been under a great deal of stress for the last eight months. Friends have noticed big changes. Lately Teresa refuses to make any optional decisions. She is still functional at work but off duty she can't (won't) make even simple decisions such as choosing between chicken and steak for dinner. She has even gone to bed without dinner on a couple of occasions just so she wouldn't have to choose what to eat!

Teresa's case may be extreme but we are all subject to psychological changes if we experience prolonged stress overload.

Mental Changes

Trevor shares, "I can always tell when I'm getting too stressed out because my memory starts to slip. I forget what I was going to say. I walk to the next room and forget what I was going to do!"

We all experience minor memory lapses but a sudden increase in the number or frequency of lapses is often a sign of excess stress. Other mental changes include decreased problem-solving capacity, difficulty in making decisions, fuzzy thinking, slowed ability to grasp (or retain) new concepts, a loss of interest in hobbies, jobs, or people, and a shortage of creative ideas.

Relational Changes

As you can easily imagine, all of the above changes in people are bound to affect their skills in relating to others. People under stress have difficulty attending, relaxing, and enjoying life. They appear preoccupied and edgy. Relaxing seems a waste of time when there are so many "more important" things that need to be done.

Because most of the stressed person's strength and energy are expended in coping with the stress, there is little left over to devote to relationships.

Spiritual Changes

"Just when I need the Lord the most, because I'm so stressed out, I seem to ignore him the most!" Dwanda admits.

A lot of us do that! Perhaps because we've found that God's timetable for us differs from the one we want to follow, we seem to push forward and take control when we begin to stress overload. We're too busy, too tired, too disinterested, or too impatient to take time out for personal devotions and prayer. We begin running on stored spiritual fuel (memorized Scriptures and remembered sermons) rather than on daily fill-ups. Soon there is a staleness in the spirit and a loss of power in daily living. It becomes easier to give in to temptation and to make poor spiritual choices.

Become familiar with the way stress affects you and learn to recognize the patterns of change that you experience. Learn to be aware of the beginning stages of stress and take corrective measures early so as to avoid the consequences of prolonged stress.

Effects of Stress on Leadership Style

"I do okay as a leader as long as things are normal, but if things get too hectic, I find that my style changes!" Cecilia confesses.

That's right! Under stress conditions, we do change our style of leadership unless we make a concerted effort not to. One common pattern is to return to a more comfortable style. Lyndel had been a take-charge, controlling manager for several years before he decided to cultivate a participative leadership style. Most of the time he uses the new style, but in a crisis or when he's under stress, he automatically reverts back to taking charge.

Another pattern is for a manager to become a worker and a leader to become a reactor. The manager's goal is to get the job done. Under stress, when no one else can or will move fast enough or do things "right," the manager will pitch in and do it him- or herself, just so the task is completed. The leader, whose strength is developing people and letting them take the lead, may become nearly immobilized and only react to extreme pressure or criticism if there is too much stress.

A third pattern, which is actually an extension of the second, is where the strengths of a particular style are carried to extremes and become weaknesses. This concept was developed by Stuart Atkins in his Life Orientation Training Program.[2] Here are some examples of how this works.

The Let's-Find-a-Compromise Person

Under normal conditions: Uses social abilities and personal charisma to cope with the work, has a youthful manner, jokes, usually isn't serious, and has a sensitivity to the needs of others.

Under stress: This person's productive qualities can become unproductive.

Productive	*Can Become*	**Unproductive**
Flexible		Inconsistent
Youthful		Childlike
Negotiating		Over-compromising
Solicitous		Fawning
Entertaining		Foolish

The Let's-Get-the-Job-Done Person

Under normal conditions: Likes to take charge, is quick to act or take a risk, seeks variety and novelty, prefers to direct and coordinate the work of others, and eagerly takes advantage of opportunities.

Under stress: This person's productive qualities can become unproductive.

Productive	*Can Become*	**Unproductive**
Controlling		Domineering
Self-confident		Arrogant
Risk taker		Gambler
Urgent		Impatient
Forceful		Coercive

The Let's-Keep-Everybody-Happy Person

Under normal conditions: Has very high standards for people, is admiring of and affirming to others, has great trust and belief in other people, is eager to respond to requests for help, is very idealistic.

Under stress: This person's productive qualities can become unproductive.

Productive	Can Become	Unproductive
Accepting		Indulgent
Trusting		Gullible
Feeling		Maudlin
Optimistic		Impractical
Thoughtful		Self-denying

The Let's-Just-Leave-One-Another-Alone-to-Do-Our-Own-Jobs Person

Under normal conditions: Has a strong reliance on logic, facts, and systems; has a need for predictability; maximizes the use of policies and procedures; doesn't like interruptions; resists change; won't participate in touchy-feely meetings.

Under stress: This person's productive qualities can become unproductive.

Productive	Can Become	Unproductive
Tenacious		Cannot let go
Factual		Data bound
Methodical		Plodding
Analytical		Critical
Realistic		Unimaginative

Recognizing what stress overload can do to us is just the first step in beginning an effective stress-management program.

Coping with Stressors

"After next Saturday, stress won't be a problem for me! I'm taking a stress management class," Chen boasts.

Unfortunately it's not that easy. Stress-management skills take time to learn. Just as it took the stress-overload situation a period of several weeks or even years to develop, so controlling the internal responses to external demands cannot be accomplished overnight. Here are some steps to follow in coping with stress.

1. Keep a written record.

Write down everything that triggers your stress response during a one-week period. Note the response and the time it took to calm down afterward. Rate each stressor on a scale of one to twenty (with twenty being strongest). At the end of a week, add up the number of times your stress response was triggered by a stressor rated between fifteen and twenty. (If the number is over ten, try to eliminate as many of these stressors as possible during the next week.)

Stressors come in all kinds of packages. Remember that any change (large or small, pleasant or unpleasant) is a stressor. What about these?

deadlines
new assignments
interruptions
unclear goals
conflicting demands
long hours of work
clutter

friend moving away
death of a friend or
   relative
pregnancy
illness
vacation
getting a traffic ticket

interpersonal conflicts
competition
new job
new home
new church
new friends
new work hours
change in recreational habits
spouse starting/stopping work
starting/quitting school
child leaving home
new family member
problem in the church
hospitalization
conflicts with in-laws
terrific personal success

being audited by the
  IRS
having things break
  down
financial shortages
rude people
holidays
noise
going on a diet
loss of sleep
fears of failing
lack of recognition
lack of affirmation
prolonged loneliness
serious personal failure

And the list goes on!

2. Set priorities.

Prioritize the stressors in your life, putting at the top of your list the ones you may be able to resolve. Give yourself permission to ignore other demands while you concentrate on these stressors. For example, give up your usual home-cooked meals two or three nights a week in favor of eating take-out food or having easy-to-prepare sandwiches. This could give you almost two extra hours on those days to do other things. For a short, specified period, deal with only priority demands. Don't try to do everything all of the time.

3. Allow God's input into your priorities.

While he has promised strength for everything we do (Phil. 4:13), he also has a few other lessons for us. Setting aside twenty to thirty minutes a day to read from God's Word and to carefully contemplate what he is saying serves to spiritually gird us up against the stressors in life. The promises are innumerable. Try these:

> But seek first his kingdom and his righteousness, and all these things will be given to you as well.
>
> Matthew 6:33

> You will keep in perfect peace him whose mind is steadfast, because he trusts in you.
>
> Isaiah 26:3

> He gives strength to the weary and increases the power of the weak. Even youths grow tired and weary, and young men stumble and fall; but those who hope in the LORD will renew their strength. They soar on wings like eagles; they will run and not grow weary, they will walk and not be faint.
>
> Isaiah 40:29–31

What a glorious promise! To have renewed strength to cope with any stressor! He is faithful.

4. Talk to God.

As important as listening to God's input is, the communication is not to be all one-sided. Share with him those hidden feelings you are afraid to voice aloud to anyone else. Tell him your fears. He understands the pain of unjust criticism, of being forgotten, of needing love. Ask for wisdom and guidance in setting priorities in your life. With his help, you can be more than a conqueror (Rom. 8:37).

5. Set up a reward system.

Whenever an intervention successfully reverses the stress response, reward yourself. The reward must be something you value and desire. For example: a new book, a new outfit, a fishing trip, or a special meal. The reward should come from yourself, not from others, although a little praise from peers is also rewarding.

6. Follow rules for good health.

The general rules for coping with stress will probably be familiar to you, for they are the basic guidelines given us by our parents, teachers, physicians, and health books for good health. If we fail to follow these rules, we compromise our body's ability to respond to and cope effectively with stress, leaving it more vulnerable to exhaustion and illness. We all know the basic rules but few of us ever realized that neglecting them could contribute to our anxiety problems. For review, these guidelines are:

- Maintain a balanced life. Some people don't balance work with play. They find it difficult to quit working and get involved in some activity for the sole purpose of enjoyment. Very active people who feel guilty about occasionally sitting around and doing nothing may need to give themselves permission to learn to loaf a little. The person who does not balance work and play does not give his body time to relax from the tensions of life. Balance is needed between mental, social, physical, and spiritual activity.

- Get enough sleep and rest. Most adults require about six to eight hours of sleep per night. A regular lack of sleep prevents the body from building up the resistance required to defend against stress and illness.

- Talk out negative feelings. Almost every article one reads about stress management extols the value of having a personal confidante. Internalizing negative feelings allows them to fester and manifest themselves in a variety of physical problems. Verbally expressing those feelings, on the other hand, gives vent to the tension and frustration that accompany them.

- Have regular physical checkups. It is important to go to one's doctor for periodic checkups. Identification of physical problems early on makes correcting them much easier. Keeping oneself fit contributes to a sense of well-being and puts one in a better position to handle routine stressors.

- Avoid self-medication. We are a nation of self-medicated people. We take tranquilizers when we feel uptight, caffeine when we're dragging, and sedatives when we can't sleep. And the people who do this are not thrill-seeking young people but responsible adults, often career professionals. While these substances seem harmless enough, the highs and lows they produce can trap a person in a never-ending cycle. At best, self-medication is only a temporary solution and at worst it can evolve into a long-term enemy and a stressor in itself.

- Maintain a healthful diet. Review the fundamentals of good nutrition and the guidelines for preparing regular, well-balanced meals. Understand the roles of vitamins and minerals in keeping the body in optimal shape to cope with unexpected tensions. Establish and follow a sensible eating plan. Reduce your fat intake. Avoid refined sugars, bleached flour, and other empty calories as much as possible, for these deplete the body of the specific vitamins (B) that are needed for coping with stress.

- Exercise. There is little doubt that most people could do with more exercise in their lives. Exercise plays a role in maintaining muscle tone, keeping the body systems functioning smoothly, and developing the ability to moderate one's physical response to unexpected stress.

Obviously none of these general rules are new. Each one is time tested and grounded in common sense. When we make an effort to understand their importance in controlling our stress responses, we may gain a new desire and commitment to incorporate them into our lifestyle.

7. Use specific interventions.

Following the general principles of effective stress management helps us develop coping strength so that new stressors do not unduly traumatize our bodies. From a position of strength we can select the specific intervention we need to moderate our responses to individual stressors. A few of the possible interventions are given below.

- Take a break.
- Learn to relax physically.
- Take a class on stress management.
- Limit the amount of work brought home from the office.
- Engage in a highly reinforcing activity—something you enjoy—when you get home from work. Work on a hobby, play with your children, chat with your spouse or a friend.
- Learn to make decisions and then let them go.
- Obtain closure on unfinished business and relationships.
- Learn to be assertive.
- Experience forgiveness and be forgiving.
- Take a day off.
- Read a book.
- Listen to soothing music.
- Go out to eat.
- Do volunteer work.
- Seek advice.

- Play with children/pets/grandchildren.
- Laugh.
- Go to church.
- Talk with a friend.
- Play a sport.
- Take a warm bath/sit in a jacuzzi.
- Swim.
- Run.
- Meditate on a favorite Scripture verse.
- Breathe deeply and slowly.
- Cry.

There are dozens of ways to moderate the stress response and to increase your coping skills in the process.

Some Stress Is Good

"I work better under pressure," Elena admits cheerfully as she collates the last-minute duplicating for the conference. She has only an hour and there are five hundred sets. She'll get it done.

Some amount of stress is good, it gets the blood pumping and the ideas flowing. Most people would be bored to tears if their lives were characterized by the unrelieved monotony of an unchanging daily routine. We need to be challenged out of our comfort zones and forced to cope with changes. Finding the right tension between boring monotony and frantic change is the ongoing challenge we live with.

Part 4

Learning
a New
Approach

Call

What If I Got Out of the Way?

My full-time job as a pastor is staying out of the way," Roger shared. "This frees the Holy Spirit to do what he wants in the people's lives as he accomplishes his work through them. It's important to resist the urge to jump in and take control."

Do you ever have impulses like that? Many people in leadership know what needs to be done and at least one good way to get it done. When people are fumbling around or procrastinating in getting a job done, it is tempting to fix things by doing the task ourselves. When this happens, we need to stop and reconfirm our calling. What is it God has placed us in ministry to do? It isn't necessarily to produce successful programs. It is the development of people.

A Call to Relationships

Our call as Christians, as well as leaders, is to be in right relationship with God, with other members of the Christian family, and with the world.

Relationship with God

In the creation account of Adam and Eve, God would come to walk in the garden with them in the cool of the day, beginning a personal relationship with the very first man and woman. That pattern has continued for nearly six thousand years. Our relationship with the Lord can be intensely personal and intimate. We are a covenant community. In Acts 2, Peter took the prophesy of Joel 2:28–32 and applied it to the experience of the Christian community, illustrating the fact that the Jewish hope had been ultimately fulfilled in Christ. We are part of a new covenant called into being by our faith in Christ.

As a covenant people, our relationship with God involves mutual commitment and response. God chooses us and we in response choose him. In Isaiah 1:18 God calls us to come to him and "reason together." In Psalm 46:10 God tells us to "Be still, and know that I am God." John 15:1–11 tells us to abide in him. He works his will through us and we can do nothing without him.

Our personal relationship with the Lord begins with our response to his love and our acceptance of his salvation. Then begins the lifelong process of becoming intimate with God. Even though our Lord has perfect knowledge of us, we often need to take our time getting to know, trust, and love him.

Knowing God

One way of getting to know God is through his written word. Reading and studying the Bible can give us perspective about God and his relationships with real people throughout history. Instructions, exhortations, and encouragements are found in the words of Scripture. Through the Bible, God meets us and we can discover his word becoming a vital part of our lives.

A second way to know God is by hearing others' stories as they share what God is doing in their lives. As we see how he loves, cares for, teaches, and empowers others, we learn more about his character and his person.

A third way to know God is to dialogue with him in prayer. When we turn our minds and hearts toward him we discover his agendas, priorities, and purposes for us.

The more we know about God, the more real and intimate our relationship with him becomes. It is said of people who are very close that each knows what the other is thinking. One of our major goals is to have the mind of Christ (Phil. 2:5). Our words, behavior, and choices can be those that Christ would have for us, if we focus on cultivating an intimate relationship with God.

Trusting God

Someone once said that we don't mind if God is the master architect as long as he gives us blueprint approval! So often we are willing to trust God with selected areas of our lives but we hold back areas that we want to control. Perhaps we fear that God might not do things our way! We often believe we know exactly how things should be done.

If there were a fortune-teller who could tell the future with absolute certainty, she would probably be the richest person in the world and impossible to see for the crowd gathered around her. People would flock to consult the fortune-teller on investments, relationships, and decisions of every kind. Even as Christians we might be tempted to seek advice. Well there is no such person but we do have a God who is all knowing. He not only knows what is best for us, he knows the consequences of the choices we make, good and bad. He has given us assurance that he wants what's best for us. Yet we are still afraid to relax and trust him.

Obeying God

Sometimes obedience is easy. If we want to do what is right and there is nothing to keep us from obeying, chances are we will do what is right. The problem arises when we know what is right and desire to do it but we have to struggle against a part of us that does not want to obey. Paul writes of this struggle in Romans 7:14–25. He says, "For the good that I wish, I do not do; but I practice the very evil that I do not wish" (v. 19 NASB).

Disobedience is sometimes rooted in our desire for instant gratification. Sometimes it can be an act of selfishness or a lack of self-discipline. Doing right when you want to just takes energy. Doing the right thing when you don't want to takes obedience and self-discipline.

Bobbie belongs to a health spa but hates to work out. She takes her spa bag to work on those days she plans to visit the club. About noon she begins to invent excuses for not going. It's too hot, too rainy, or too late; she feels sick or tired. If she can, she will avoid going. However, when she does go, she loves having gone! Exercising self-discipline is tough, but it feels good having done it.

Acknowledging the call to obedience is a daily choice. We don't decide once and for all that we will obey; we are faced many times each day with choices that challenge our obedience. That's where trust comes in. If we trust God to be everything he promises to be, we can rely on that knowledge to give us the strength to obey his commands.

Loving God

"We sing a lot of songs about loving God, but I'm not sure we mean them," Brandon admits. "It's an awesome thing to love God!"

True. When we first enter a relationship with Christ, there can be a tremendous rush of love for the Lord that lights our faces and permeates every aspect of our lives. It's a wonderful form of infatuation. Like infatuation for another person, though, it can die out if we don't get to know, trust, and love that person over time. On the other hand the infatuation we may feel for a person can grow into love as we spend time getting to know that person intimately. The same is true for our relationship with God. The more we get to know him, the more we trust him; and the more we obey him, the more we will love him.

Relationships with Fellow Believers

"If it weren't for the people, we could have a terrific ministry," Tonya jokes. Therein lies the crux of our calling. We aren't called to create well-running machines or organizations; we are called to walk together, to fellowship, to edify, and to equip one another for the sharing of the good news that God loves people and wants an intimate relationship with them (Heb. 10:25; 1 John 1:7; Eph. 4:2–15).

If it were that easy to love one another, then Christian love wouldn't be an issue of obedience. The Lord knows it isn't easy to get to know, trust, support, and love one another. His own disciples were not an instantly loving group. They argued among themselves and even sought status over one another. Learning to love people in spite of their faults is a process we undertake in the power of the Holy Spirit.

Loving people can change them. There was a lady who came to the singles ministry at a large church. People avoided her because she was so consistently negative. She complained about everything and gossiped about others. Her face wore a perpetual frown. Although the leader was tempted to ignore her, he knew that underneath that prickly exterior lived a person whom God loved. The leader went out of his way to speak with her each week, to sit in her discussion group, and to ask her about her week. Her initial response was predictably negative, but the leader persisted. A few of the people were deliberately seeking this lady out each week and showing her Christian love. Within a few months the protective shield dropped and she stopped being so critical, bitter, and negative. She risked trusting a few people and in time began to develop a new outlook.

Everyone needs love, even those who really aren't comfortable with intimacy. We are called to love one another and to risk trusting them with intimacy. We must be aware that in the process, we will probably be let down, betrayed, and hurt as often as we are affirmed, encouraged, and cared for. That's because we aren't perfect and we live in a world of broken trust. In such a world love is possible and the community is sustained and strengthened through forgiveness.

Sharing Our Faith in the World

Frank Tillapaugh points out that nowhere in the Bible does it say that the world must go to church. It says the church must go to the world (Matt. 28:19–20). If we are to share our faith, we must be willing to go out to the everyday world and live in the power of the Holy Spirit, letting people see what God is doing in our lives. We cannot reach the world alone; we need the help of other believers. This means that we dare not restrict the outreach by trying to control the ministry. We must release people to go out and minister in the world as they make their dreams come alive.

A Call to Get Out of the Way

"We have so many excuses for not relinquishing control," Gustav shares. "And they're good reasons, too!"

He's right. We do have a lot of excuses we use as reasons to hold on to the control of the ministry. The following are just a small sample:

- Their ideas won't work.
- There are other priorities.
- Others tried something similar and failed.
- There's not enough time.
- The time's not right.
- It costs too much.
- It's not the way we do things here.
- I'm too tired to train someone else.
- I don't know how.
- I can't.

When we make ourselves the conduit through which all ministry must pass, we limit the ministries that can occur. They are limited by our time, our energies, and our other priorities. But if we are ready to break out of the role of controller and see what God can do, there is no limit to what he can accomplish through us. Here are some steps to help.

Recognize that it is his ministry. How foolish it would be if a motorist with a small portable fire extinguisher saw three cars burning on the freeway and was so determined to put out the fires himself that he wouldn't get out of the way of the fire engine headed for the accident. Is it any different when we attempt to do the job of running a ministry ourselves instead of getting out of the way of the Holy Spirit?

Release our expectations so he can work. Our ideas are limited, but the Holy Spirit has unlimited ideas and knows which ones will work. If we set him free to work, then people will be reached beyond our limited abilities.

Allow room for miracles. As long as we stick only to that which we are sure will succeed, we aren't depending on the miraculous power of God in our ministries. We should frequently step out in faith, trusting God to provide what is needed as we follow the leading of the Spirit. This is not to say we should be foolhardy or reckless with the Lord's resources but it does mean we need to give God room to work.

Our success is not only in the results we have in ministry, not only in the success we see in other people, but also in what is happening inside ourselves. We change as we trust people and take risks in relationships. We grow. We become more like Christ, which is one of God's goals for us.

Climate

When Are We Ready?

agree with everything you've said about leadership and I'm ready to change my whole approach to ministry," Drake says. "My problem is that I'm only one of three associate pastors and the others may not go along with me on this. How do I know when we're ready to start the new approach?"

Good question. Answer: There is no "right time"! Therefore, the time to change is now. There will be many obstacles even if everyone involved agrees with the planned changes. Some obstacles will be harder to overcome than others. If the other staff members, the church board, or the congregation are not aware of or in agreement with the new approach, the changes will take place more slowly and take more time and energy to implement.

Possible Obstacles

Here are some of the bigger obstacles you may face.

A Focus on Numbers

"The first question anyone asks after a special event is how many attended," Marita says sadly. "Numbers are great but results in the lives of people are better. Results are what count."

When success is measured solely in terms of numbers and when results are only important if they can be easily quantified, then changing from a managing style to a leading style will probably meet with some resistance. Eventually the leading style will reach more people but initially the numbers of people attending your church program may not significantly increase. That is because you are focusing on developing the people you have and not necessarily on bringing in more people.

You can tell that numbers are important when leaders are required to file only statistical reports and are commended only for numerical growth.

Forced Dishonesty

There are some churches where it is not always acceptable to be honest about shortcomings and mistakes regarding motives, activities, and performance. Where failures must always be explained away and spiritualized by phrases like, "God must be wanting to teach me a lesson in this area." God may have a lesson for us to learn through certain failures, but some failures occur simply because someone chose an unworkable alternative. We need a working climate where we can say, "I messed up."

Follow Me

Some leaders insist that their people do everything in a prescribed manner. They leave no room for creativity, innovation, or change. If you work in ministry with and report to a leader such as this, you will experience great difficulty in making a drastic change in your approach to ministry until that leader is converted to the new approach.

Power Games

Very often the political climate within a church involves numerous and predictable power games. Some games include It's-no-good-unless-it's-my-idea; You-can-do-it-as-long-as-I'm-in-control; I'll-say-I'll-support-you-but-won't-come-through; and Don't-ever-cross-me.

If you work with a person who must be in total control and who wants to keep all the power, you will have a hard time changing your style. While a manager gets somewhat involved in power struggles in order to achieve his or her goals, a leader only uses his or her power to equip and empower others.

Changing the Climate

Regardless of the climate in your church, you needn't be stopped from beginning to choose a new approach to ministry.

Influence Change

The terrific thing about life is that we can change not only our minds, our attitudes, and our behaviors but also the climate in which we work. Our attitudes and our behaviors affect those people around us. Perhaps you've heard about the man who told a friend to walk behind him and to closely watch the faces of the next five people who walked toward them. After five people had approached and passed them, the man asked his friend to comment. "They were all angry looking and scowling," his friend observed.

They resumed walking once again. When five more people had approached and passed them the man asked again for his friend's observations. When his friend replied that "these were much nicer people, they were all smiling and pleasant," the man explained that he had scowled and frowned angrily at the first five as they came toward him and smiled and nodded pleasantly to the second five.

Life is not quite as easy to manipulate by simply frowning and smiling but it is often true that the way we treat people will influence the responses we get from them. When considering a different leadership approach it is helpful to first talk with those who might oppose it and discuss the issues together. Find out what their fears or oppositions are and see if you can agree on ways to meet their needs as well as obtain the freedom you need to try a new style.

Sometimes you may have to use the old style in some of your ministry (to keep those in authority over you happy) and try the new approach in one or two areas (to keep you happy). As your success with the new approach becomes apparent perhaps you can win over the opposition.

Prayer

None of us is wise enough or strong enough to effect major changes on our own strength. We need the guidance and power of the Holy Spirit to not only lead the way, but also to work in the hearts of other people. Our prayers for change must be comprehensive and include the willingness to be changed ourselves when that is needed.

Even though we have a good idea, we may take the wrong approach. We may be impatient. We may be insensitive in our presentation or arguments. We may need to be tempered, toned down, or taught to enlist cooperation rather than trying to coerce people. Part of our prayer then is for the Holy Spirit to search our hearts and see if there are any changes that need to be made (see Psalm 139:23–24).

A second aspect of our prayer time is seeking God's wisdom and insight. We were promised in James 1:5 that if we ask, we will receive the wisdom we need. Who better than God to help us know what to say and when to say it?

Standing Firm

We may need the perseverance to be patient, strong, and undiscourageable! Often leaders fail, not because they were incapable or because the climate was unchangeable, but because they gave up too soon. We need the power to keep on keeping on. Paul says in Ephesians 6:13 "put on the full armor of God, so that when the day of evil comes, you may be able to stand your ground, and after you have done everything, to stand."

Don't be afraid to cling to good ideas and goals regardless of the opposition. This doesn't mean forcing others to agree or go along with you immediately. It means not giving up on the ideas prematurely. There is, however, sometimes a point when even "good" ideas are shelved because the timing just isn't right.

Part of standing firm is learning to work within the climate. When Jacob moved from sunny southern California to rainy Seattle he was surprised to see picnics scheduled on the church calendar. "How can you plan a picnic here?" he asked a member of the church. "What if it rains?"

"If it rains," the member replied, "we work around the weather."

If you don't give up on picnics just because you live in a rainy climate, how much more important is it not to give up on ideas because someone doesn't embrace them right away!

Being Patient

"At first I was really upset when most of the church board didn't go along with my ideas for releasing the people into more individual ministries," Juan admits. "But in the following months I discovered that I was fine-tuning my dreams and ideas and getting prepared for when we did start using a different approach. Actually now that I look back on it, the delay was really good."

Our idea may be a good one but the timing may be bad. In Acts 1:4 we read that the apostles were told to wait until they had been empowered by the Holy Spirit. How often do we rush out and try to force away the obstacles, thinking that Satan is blocking us, when in reality it is the Lord's hand that is gently holding us back until we or others are ready and the time is right?

When the time is right the support will be available and there will be leaders emerging for the people to put the ministry in motion. Trying to force a ministry before its time often results in a premature birth for the dream and a shaky start at best.

We can sense the time is right when the need is perceived by more than one person, when people emerge as willing leaders for the new ministry, and when there is a proper mix of opportunity and desire.

Waiting can be frustrating if we are looking for quick, numerical results. But if we keep in mind that our goal is developing people, we can remember that the process takes time and we can wait more easily.

Changing the Ministry

"One day I felt the time was right, so I went into the office and outlined several changes I'd like to see in our ministry," Harold says. "I'd waited for almost a year and had talked individually with most of the staff. I decided there was no time like the present to begin!"

Start now. Harold has a point. There is no time like now to make changes and to begin moving in a new direction. There is never a perfect time, completely free from obstacles. While we mustn't forge out so far ahead of people that they feel lost, we needn't wait for every single person to agree with us before we take the first step. When there is support, and people are willing to at least try something new, you can start.

Look for alternatives. If we can't use the new approach within the current church structure, we can use it outside. Not all ministries have to be "validated" by being sponsored by a church. Individuals can help street people, counsel the brokenhearted, and reach out to underprivileged neighborhood children.

Don't ask permission. "I've found that if I wait for official permission for everything I want to do, I'll be doing very little. So I often just go ahead and minister and then share the excitement of the success of the new ministry in the next staff meeting," Lynn says. (Note: This approach won't work with every church. Rebels or innovators often find themselves unemployed!)

Don't belittle others. When making changes we must be careful not to make others feel belittled because they choose to use a different approach to leadership. Various approaches will work; we just happen to believe that the leading approach works best.

Become comfortable with ambiguity. "You really don't ever become totally capable," Alicia asserts, "you just become more comfortable with ambiguity."

She's right. We don't have to be perfect to do effective ministry. You won't always know what's going on. You won't be in total control. At times you will feel powerless. There will be days when you won't be sure what you've accomplished. Learn to accept these uncomfortable consequences and celebrate the real results, the people who have become strong ministers to others.

Sometimes You Leave

"How long do you stay in a church when it appears that there will never be a time when things are going to change?" Steven asks.

That's hard to say. First, we don't know that things will never change, because we cannot predict the future. Second, each situation is different. Sometimes you stay; sometimes you leave.

Maybe our role in a particular ministry is time limited. Paul says that some may plant and others may water, but God is responsible for the results (1 Cor. 3:5–8). Maybe we have been called to plant the seed and then move on. The next person may "nurture" the ideas and eventually growth will occur.

Perhaps we are the only one who wants a different approach and everyone else is happy with the current style of ministry. If there is absolutely no receptiveness, we may choose to look for another ministry, where our dreams and our style are more acceptable.

Maybe God is moving us out to a new calling. We need to be sensitive to his leading and neither jump too quickly nor stay too long. Only God knows what's ahead for us. If we trust him implicitly, Proverbs 3:6 says, "he will make your paths straight."

Cost

What Is the Bottom Line?

I f I decide to change my ministry style and be more of a leader, then I may need to consider what the changes will cost me personally," Calvin says thoughtfully. "I guess I'd have to take a close look at the bottom line. I'm not sure that the choice would be all that easy!"

A Look at the Price Tag

There is a certain price tag on choosing to be a leader who gives people the freedom to fulfill their dreams of ministry.

Loss of Control

After spending our lives fighting for control, we must make a deliberate choice to relinquish control. We need to learn to feel comfortable not having total control, because as long as we are in control, the ministry will remain small enough to be managed by us. As we let go, we soon learn to fail and to give others the freedom to fail as well. When we fail, or when others fail, we risk our reputations and we may be labeled as failures. This can be intimidating but we must learn to see failure not as an end but as a stepping-stone to success.

The benefits to relinquishing control are several. The body of Christ is strengthened as more of the individual members are empowered to go forth and minister to one another and to the world. Individual people have multiple opportunities to grow and to develop new skills and ministries. You are free to see the big picture of the total ministry rather than getting a distorted perception because you are too close to the details. And the creative ideas, the ministry and outreach, grow exponentially as more and more people get involved.

Loss of Information

"Sometimes I feel as if I'm the most uninformed person in the church," one associate pastor shared. "I once got a call asking where the unemployed support group met on Monday mornings. I told the caller that we didn't have a group like that, perhaps it was at another church. The caller insisted that the group existed and claimed he had seen the notice in the Sunday bulletin. Determined to prove my point I reached for my copy of the bulletin and there was the notice of the group! I quickly gave him the information and hung up the phone."

It turns out that a few of the unemployed church members had decided to get up on Monday mornings, get dressed, gather up their resumes, and get out of the house. So they reserved a room at the church and started meeting early on Monday mornings before going out to look for work. They never thought of asking permission to start a "ministry"—they were just getting together to help each other. The senior pastor knew about the group but hadn't mentioned it to the staff.

As more and more people are included in the dreaming process, you will equip and empower more people and you will not always be the one who has all the information about the ministry. You just won't be able to be kept informed of all the details. You may feel left out, abandoned, and unimportant. With the loss of information comes a decrease in power because information is a major source of power. You may experience feelings of isolation and loneliness. That is just all part of the cost.

The benefits of not serving as the main source of information are many. The people will be talking more to one another, which promotes teamwork, fellowship, and intimacy. More people will be actively involved in the flow of information and consequently more people will be empowered. If all of the information doesn't have to flow through one person, there is no bottleneck to slow down the ministry.

Lack of Easily Measurable Results

There are some very definite results from using the leading approach to ministry but they aren't as easy to count or record on a statistical chart as numbers are. Therefore if we aren't very clear about what we are striving for, we can become easily discouraged and believe that we are not successful. If attendance is down, we may feel that we should scrap everything and try something else. We may experience a loss of self-esteem because on the surface our ministry may not be the biggest and brightest. We may not receive the credit or recognition we deserve for our ministries because we may not have all of the fancy programs other churches do. We may be criticized for not managing, for not doing more ourselves. This approach costs.

There are many benefits to not pushing for easily measurable results. Each time we do not personally take charge and do something, we are giving other people opportunities to minister. We are forced to set very specific people-related goals for our ministries. We learn to differentiate between our job (to be an enabler) and an opportunity for ministry (e.g., serving food to single-parent families). We come to a place where we aren't pointing to the numbers, trying to prove our worth. And, of course, we aren't tempted to go around bragging about our bigger and better ministry.

Don't misunderstand when we refer to managed ministries as being bigger. We believe that led ministries will truly be more extensive and farther reaching because more people are out touching others and ministering. It's just that in a managed ministry, the emphasis is usually on having fewer meetings and getting as many people as possible together. For some reason, we have traditionally been more impressed with two hundred people attending one general meeting than with twenty small groups of ten people meeting at various locations. In a led ministry you may have twenty things happening around the city and in homes, with five to ten people attending each.

Loss of Instant Gratification

"When I used to judge my success by the programs I developed, I got a lot of immediate satisfaction when the programs came together and all went well," Jessica admits. "Now that I see my goal as helping people develop, it takes a lot longer to see results!"

People do develop slowly and it often takes a lot of patience to walk their journey with them, at their pace. There is more pain when a person fails to develop than when one of our programs fails. We can become frustrated and feel uncomfortable in our new role when we no longer have our hands on everything, because we are letting others have the satisfaction of doing the actual ministry.

There are several benefits to not striving for immediate satisfaction. When the reward does come it can be tremendous. What a thrill it is to see one of our people grow and develop strength in the Lord to do something that had once been impossible for him or her. The reward, though delayed, is very significant because it represents an eternal return on our investment in the lives of our people. Through this process people discover their calling as leaders and ministers and change from being takers to being givers.

Being Uncomfortable

Whenever you experiment with a new behavior style, the first experiences are generally uncomfortable. We feel awkward because the behavior is unfamiliar and we aren't skilled in the new approach. We are sure that everyone is watching and waiting to mock us or laugh at our mistakes. Our self-esteem suffers. We may be misunderstood, be called "impractical," be criticized, and experience a lack of support and approval. Add to this the fact that our adopting a leading approach to ministry will probably make some of our people uncomfortable and unhappy and ensure that we don't live up to the expectations of a few.

There is substantial compensation, however, for this temporary discomfort. If we are uncomfortable, it usually means that we have stretched out of our comfort zone and are growing and developing new skills and abilities. Our stretching becomes an example and an inspiration to others, encouraging them to grow. We generally become more versatile, more skilled, and more capable. We also may develop a greater trust in God as we depend more on his guidance and approval than on that of people. We become less focused on pleasing people and we develop greater sufficiency.

Counting the Cost

There is a freeway bridge in northern California that stood for years in the middle of a field, unconnected at either end to a freeway. The funds appropriated for connecting two freeways were only sufficient to build the huge bridge. There it stood, a silent mockery to those who failed to correctly count the cost.

On Catalina Island a housing development went unfinished for two and a half years when the developer ran out of money after framing the houses. The wooden beams began to warp from prolonged exposure to the weather. A tragedy of miscalculated cost.

Jesus said that wise people sit down and count the cost before they start something (Luke 14:28–30). When starting a new approach, think it through first. Consider what you might expect to happen. Trust God to empower you to see it through until it begins to work and people are comfortable with it.

Depending on the situation the cost may seem too great at first. If this happens, take smaller steps. Rethink and reconsider to ensure that you have developed an accurate estimate of the situation. Get a second opinion. Talk over all of the pros and cons with a trusted friend. This will help you check your perception of the total situation. If the big dream is still too costly in your particular situation, then scale down the dream a step or two and start small. If you absolutely must delay making a change, remember it is just a delay and not a cancellation. Then, while you wait, learn to cope with some of the anticipated consequences of making a change.

Count the cost but don't be afraid to pay for the change. It's worth everything you pay and as such it is still definitely a bargain!

16

Challenge

Where Do I Start?

an's first year as minister to single adults was amazing! He worked night and day, building the single adult program into a huge success. They had Bible studies, small groups, outreach, socials, service projects, specialized ministries (divorce recovery, single-parenting seminars, and grief recovery), and even a newsletter. In order to ensure success, Jan did most of the work. He retained control of most aspects of the program. He started out being a manager and ended up being a worker because he thought people weren't as committed to the success of the program as he was. He found himself getting more and more exhausted and discouraged. Finally he admitted to himself that he just couldn't keep up the pace. He went to the board of elders intending to tender his resignation. "I feel like a failure here," Jan started, "I just can't do everything that's required to have such a successful program."

One of the elders smiled. "We wondered when you would figure that out! We don't want you to burn yourself out. Look around the room, we're all unable to do everything that needs to be done. Leaders soon learn that the work of the ministry is best done by the people." Heads nodded in agreement as Jan looked around the room. He began to realize that the purpose of ministry is reaching and enabling people, not building programs. He began to catch a new vision of an old philosophy and suddenly knew he couldn't quit. He would change instead.

Psychologists tell us that people change when the present becomes more painful to endure than the fear of the consequences of change. As long as we are comfortable with the status quo, we seldom change. We usually have to be prodded to decide to make major changes. Jan had come to the point of change and asked himself, "Where do I start?"

The "Cold-Turkey" Change

After a couple of weeks of planning and praying about making a change in his style of leadership, Jan chose his strategy. Knowing his own need for control, he knew he wouldn't be able to let go gradually. He would have to change cold turkey.

After teaching the singles class the next Sunday morning, he had a few words to say to the group. "I want to thank you for a wonderful year," he started. "We've had a lot of fun together and done a lot of great things. Thank you, all. However, it's over now. This is the last Sunday of our single adult program." Jan stepped down off the platform while the singles sat in stunned silence.

"Wait!" one man called out. "What do you mean it's over? It can't be over. We don't want the program to be over."

"Yeah," another single piped up. "What if we don't want it to be over?"

"Well," Jan said thoughtfully, "I don't know. What could you do if you didn't want the singles ministry to stop?"

"We could keep it going ourselves," one woman suggested.

"We could get together and come up with a plan," another woman chimed in.

"Yes, you could do that," Jan agreed, trying not to smile. "You could even meet at the church one night to decide what you want to do!"

After a bit more general discussion, one of the men stood up and announced that there would be a planning meeting on Wednesday night at seven o'clock at the church.

Jan was nervous all week wondering what was going to happen. One of the hardest things he had ever done was to stay away from the church on that Wednesday night. This was the test. Either the people would own the ministry and run with it or the ministry would die.

No one called him on Thursday to report on the meeting. He was dying to know what happened. He almost asked the janitor if the room had been messed up so that he'd know if anyone even showed up for the planning meeting. But he didn't. He waited.

Finally on Friday one of the singles called and reported. There had been thirteen attendees. They had reviewed the entire singles program, deciding which things they wanted to maintain (most of them) and which to stop (only a couple). People had grouped themselves into work teams to take responsibility for the different aspects of the existing program. Within a couple of hours the mantle had been passed and a new leadership structure was in place.

"The people have been running the single adult program ever since, and that was five years ago," Jan says. "My hardest job is still making myself get out of the way so the people can be unleashed to do what God has envisioned for them and empowered them to do."

Benefits of a Cold-Turkey Change

There are several benefits to making a sudden change. First, there is shock value. People are startled out of complacency and virtually forced to react and make changes. Second, the results are immediate and noticeable, which can be very rewarding.

Risks of a Cold-Turkey Change

A cold-turkey change brings with it several risks, which must be considered.

First, there may be chaos if there are not people who are ready to assume leadership roles, or the wrong people try to assume leadership. Also, since you are removed from the center of the ministry, you may find that your own dreams are abandoned as the people's dreams take priority. The changeover may be disappointing if the people do not rally together and support one another. If the new leaders tend to be managers instead of leaders, they may stifle the growth of the ministry by not releasing the people and by failing to equip and empower more leaders. Inevitably the ministry will change directions and the church will change. And depending on the long-term results of the change, you may be out of a job.

Planning a Cold-Turkey Change

To be effective, a cold-turkey change must be carefully planned!

Be sure you hurt enough to change. Don't go for a drastic change unless you are absolutely unwilling to tolerate the status quo any longer, regardless of the risks of such a change. If you are not sure, then you may be tempted to abandon the change when the going gets rough.

Know where you are headed with the change. You will want to be very clear about what you hope to accomplish and what response you expect. Jan had been pretty sure his people would rally together and take over the ministry when they were faced with the alternative of disbanding the program. There are, of course, no guarantees of how people are going to respond, but with prayer and careful planning, you can come reasonably close to predicting the outcome.

Make a total commitment to the change. Jan had hoped that the people would respond to his approach but he was prepared to follow through on his commitment even if the program were terminated. Consider all the disadvantages of retaining the status quo against the risks of sudden change, and if this is still the direction you want to go, make a total commitment. Don't be tentative or make false starts. You should be willing to fail if the change does not work but not to fail because of faulty strategy or lack of commitment.

Get support from one or two key people. Before you implement a drastic change, discuss your plan with and get support from a few key people. If you are an associate pastor or a lay leader, discuss the change with the senior pastor and church leaders. If you are the senior pastor, discuss the change with the church board. This ensures that you will have the benefit of considered thought and caring feedback before you act. Other people in leadership need to know ahead of time what your intent is and that the change has been carefully planned.

The cold-turkey method works. It entails more risks than making incremental changes but the rewards can be greater and more immediate.

The "One-Step-at-a-Time" Change

When Joel came to his church there wasn't a singles program and there were only five single adults in the congregation. He began slowly, drawing all five of the singles into the ministry. Joel had visions of what he wanted the ministry to look like and began studying effective single adult ministries. He knew that as soon as possible he wanted the people to own the ministry. But first, he had to get a ministry started.

At the beginning Joel was sometimes a worker. At other times he was a manager, but in his heart his goal was always to be a leader. As he was able, he worked individually with each of his singles, helping them develop confidence and a vision for the ministry. Whenever one would make a commitment, Joel would celebrate and step out of the way, letting the leadership expand. As more singles joined the ministry, the circle of potential leaders grew and he was able to turn more of the ministry over to the people. The transfer of power took a few years. However, Joel's success was proven when the lay leaders were able to continue the ministry long after Joel left, almost without a hitch. They had been doing it all along.

Benefits of a One-Step-at-a-Time Change

There are benefits of making incremental changes as opposed to drastic changes. First, sometimes it is the clear choice when drastic changes won't work! When the changes are gradual, they are less threatening and there is an opportunity for more acceptance by those affected. If you are making incremental changes, you can spend the time required for each step to be successful before moving on. You can even step backward a step or two if necessary from time to time. The risks are lessened and there is more of a chance for success. And you seldom lose your job as a result of making gradual changes.

Risks of a One-Step-at-a-Time Change

There are also a few risks in making changes slowly. First, the total change seems to take forever and you may lose your support base or even your own enthusiasm if too much time passes. Also, each new step offers an opportunity for someone to challenge your direction and stop your progress. The energy drain can be significant. Some of the people may find themselves stuck at the interim steps, never achieving complete change.

Planning a One-Step-at-a-Time Change

Even a gradual series of changes must be carefully planned so that the direction and strategy are clear.

Assess the status quo. Recognize what is working well and identify areas where the current style or program could use some work. This is the best way to start because you will need those affected by the change to agree that change is necessary.

Map out the long-range plan. Prioritize all of the areas of the ministry in which changes will be made over the long range. Develop a strategy for how you will implement the changes one at a time.

Make a commitment to the changes. Even if you are willing to allow the changes to evolve over a period of time, you will want to ensure that you are committed to effecting the change. Your eventual success will depend on the level of your commitment.

Get the support you need. In the slower, incremental change method, you will not only need the support of key people but also that of the people most affected by the changes.

You will want to take the time to thoroughly explain your plans for change, the benefits of the new approach, and the rationale behind your strategy. Be prepared to sell your vision to the people.

The incremental change method is sometimes the best approach to take in certain situations. The rewards come over a longer period of time but the risks are fewer.

Things to Consider

In each of the five areas of leadership covered in the self-assessment tool at the front of this book, there are several things to consider before making a change in leadership style.

Philosophy

The first step in making a change is to clarify your current philosophy and then to redefine it or refine it so that your philosophy is appropriate to the changes you intend to make.

- Write out your current philosophy of ministry.
- Read several books and articles on leadership.
- Write out what assumptions you make about people and their abilities/skills/desires to minister.
- Chart out how you currently spend the time you devote to the ministry.
- Review your current goals for the ministry.
- Decide where you want to make changes in any of the above items.
- Write out the changes in philosophy, beliefs, goals, and priorities you wish to make.

- Discuss these with and get support from the pastor/staff/congregation/board as appropriate.

Planning

Planning is key in making changes in leadership style and in the implementing of new ministries or the refining of existing programs. If you are making a switch from manager to leader, your planning process for the ministry will also change. You will want to:

- Involve more people in the planning meetings by opening up the invitation to participate and personally inviting people to attend.
- Ask questions during the meeting that will invite people to voice their opinions and share their dreams.
- Allow sufficient time for the planning meetings so that people won't feel rushed or stifled.
- Share the philosophy of ministry at each planning session so that people are aware of the intent of the planning and can see how the plans will be in line with the purpose.
- Stay out of the discussion sometimes so that the creativity will flow freely.
- Assist the planning process when it gets bogged down but only enough to get it back on track again.
- Train the people as needed.
- Facilitate the problem-solving process by giving information and support as appropriate so the plans become feasible.
- Affirm the people for participating and for developing workable plans.

Organizing

There are many ways to organize your leaders for effective ministry. You will need to review your current organizational structure to see if it will facilitate or inhibit your desired changes. If it facilitates the process, don't change it. If it will inhibit the changes, design a new organizational chart. You will want to:

- Consider the leaders you currently have in place to determine if they will support the changes.
- Check the flow of communication. Is it free enough to support the changes?
- Review who meets with whom and who is included in certain meetings (planning, evaluation, and so on).
- Review the decision-making points. Are there too many or too few to facilitate the expansion of ministry?
- Review the procedures you have in place to see which need to be changed to allow for increased creativity and ministry.
- Consider the titles you are using in your ministry. Do they exclude people instead of including them in the leadership process (e.g., only "directors" attend planning meetings, not the "coordinators" of various events)?
- Involve staff in developing their duty statements and performance expectations.
- Recognize when the other roles of reacting, working, and managing are appropriate and necessary.
- Be creative with your organizational chart. Try to expand the number of people involved in each

area. Reduce the number of levels to eliminate un-necessary bureaucracy.

Implementing

The proof of the success of the change in leadership style comes at the implementing stage of the process. Often pastors or lay leaders say they have the proper philosophy, have involved people in the planning process, and have developed a workable organization process. But if things don't begin to happen on schedule, some leaders jump in and take back the control. To ensure that you are leading at the implementing stage, you will want to:

- Recruit leaders for new ministries.
- Provide training to leaders as needed.
- Provide access for the leaders to the resources they will need to implement the ministry.
- Ensure at the planning and organizing stages that people are very clear about their roles, responsibilities, and time frames.
- Ensure that people involved in the implementation have agreed to their roles, responsibilities, and time frames.
- Ensure that people have considered things that might go wrong and have developed contingency plans of their own.
- Check the natural impulse you may have to rescue or to jump in and do it yourself.
- Allow people the freedom to improvise, experiment, succeed, or fail.
- Get out of the way of your people and their dreams.

Evaluating

Evaluating is a key step in determining the success of the ministry. Don't make the mistake of evaluating the ministry in terms of how close it comes to your dream. Remember that a ministry's success is based on its ability to develop strong believers who minister to people. As a group:

- Share in the evaluation process.
- Review the goals of the ministry and the degree to which each goal has been met.
- Affirm one another on the success attained.
- Evaluate each other to note the positive changes you have made in yourselves and in your relationships.
- Affirm these changes.
- Set developmental goals for each person in areas where growth is still needed.
- Determine adjustments needed in the ministry to further meet the stated goals.
- Avoid criticism and negativity. See problems as challenges to overcome, not failures for which to blame people.

Where do you start? Start wherever you are right now. Decide whether a drastic change or an incremental change is what will work best for your situation. Take stock. Plan. Pray. And then begin.

Part 5

Realizing
Your
Dreams

17

Success

What Is Next on the Horizon?

ince I've changed to the leadership style of ministry, I find that I'm constantly surprised by what God is doing in and through ordinary people. Every day I just consider what's next on the horizon!" one pastor says excitedly.

Anything could be on the horizon as we realize the incredible potential of releasing more and more people to minister in the power of the Holy Spirit. True success is not a destination; it is a journey toward an ever expanding ministry and outreach. Each life we touch as leaders starts a new circle of influence, much like the rippling circles created by tossing pebbles into a pond. As each person starts his or her own circle of influence, we are freed to move on, including more people in a perpetually expanding ministry.

If we remember that our goal is to develop people, then we see people as the product of our ministry. People are the validation and the proof of the effectiveness of the ministry. We will rejoice more over the development of people than over the success of a program. Our greatest joy can be to see people develop love, peace, patience, gentleness, goodness, faith, meekness, and self-control as they mature in the Lord (see Gal. 5:22–23).

If we remember that developing people is our goal, our horizons are broadened. There are always more people to reach, more people to develop, and more people to inspire to dream their dreams. The opportunities are endless. There are no limits and no boundaries.

If we remember that developing people is our real objective, then we become fulfilled as they grow in their faith and in their love for each other and in their involvement in the world.

If helping other people realize their dreams is our function, then our journey will be exciting and forever new as we become involved in the various dreams of the people we reach. We will be stretched and developed by those we are developing. *We* are people; *we* are part of the product as we ourselves develop new skills and increase our knowledge.

If we believe that what we grasp, we will lose, but what we use or give away, we will keep (see Luke 9:23–25), then we will be more likely to freely release the control and power of the ministry. What we give away leaves room for us to receive more in return.

If we remember that the ministry is not ours, that it is God's, we will be more inclined to give it back to him to use according to his purposes. Philippians 1:6 says that we can be confident that he who began a good work in us will bring it to completion.

The Choice

If you're ever in South Burlington, Vermont, be sure to visit the Ben & Jerry's ice cream factory, which ranks among the top three gourmet ice cream companies in the United States. On the tour they tell the story of the company, which was started by two men (Ben and Jerry). When the company had grown to the point where it needed to ensure that it was running at maximum efficiency, a director of quality control was hired.

The director of quality control was responsible for checking the recipes, increasing factory efficiency, testing the product, and eliminating problems within the production line. The company began to live with efficiency. The product was superb and people loved the ice cream.

But one day Ben and Jerry surveyed the company and decided that their employees weren't having any fun. So they hired a director of joy, whose responsibility it was to increase the joy within the company and the community. Some of the innovations included:

- allowing every employee to take home free ice cream
- sponsoring community festivals
- sponsoring "free-ice-cream-days" in local malls
- installing stereos and speakers on the production floor

The director of joy made an incredible difference in the company. The quality remained high as the joy increased.

We can each choose to be not only directors of quality control but also directors of joy in our ministries.

What Is Success?

Success is choosing today, right now, to make decisions about how tomorrow can be a new and better day in our ministry as we develop people—not programs—for his glory.

> Looking back in the mirror
> I see a shadowy image
> Its tentative lines
> tracing the limits
> of yesterday.
> The reality of today
> springs from yesterday's shadows—
> drawing shape,
> form,
> and reason
> from tomorrow's dreams.
> In each today
> lie seeds for tomorrow
> I choose to grow
> the ones I need
> to become my person
> for the new day.
>
> By Dottie Odell
> Used by Permission

Notes

Chapter 5: *Management*

1. James D. Anderson and Ezra Earl Jones, *The Management of Ministry* (New York: Harper & Row, 1978), 80.

Chapter 6: *Myths*

1. Gifford Pinchot III, *Intrapreneuring* (New York: Harper & Row, 1985).

Chapter 7: *Motivation*

1. Harry Levinson, *The Great Jackass Fallacy* (Boston: Harvard College, 1973), 10.

2. Douglas McGregor, *The Human Side of Enterprise* (New York: McGraw Hill, 1960).

Chapter 12: *Distress*

1. Dr. Hans Selye, *Stress without Distress* (Philadelphia: J. P. Lippencott, 1974).
2. Li Fo Associates. Stuart Atkins, Inc., 1967.

About the Authors

Bobbie Reed is author of over thirty books as well as curricula, magazine columns, and articles. Her work has included hospital administration, management consulting, as well as serving as a chief deputy warden for a state prison in California. She earned her Ph.D. from University of Central California and D. Min. from Northern Baptist Theological Seminary. She is widely known as a speaker and consultant.

John Westfall serves as a senior pastor in California. He's a popular speaker at retreats and conferences. He has served as the host of a radio program and is known as the author of *Coloring outside the Lines* and *Enough Is Enough*.